Indestructible

THE UNFORGETTABLE MEMOIR OF A MARINE HERO AT THE BATTLE OF IWO JIMA

Jack H. Lucas with D. K. Drum

WILLIAM MORROW
An Imprint of HarperCollins*Publishers*

HarperCollins books may be purchased for educational, business, or sales promotional use. For information, please email the Special Markets Department at SPsales@harpercollins.com.

Unless otherwise noted, all insert photographs are courtesy of the author.

Originally published by Da Capo Press in 2006.

FIRST WILLIAM MORROW PAPERBACK EDITION PUBLISHED 2020.

Designed by Diahann Sturge

Library of Congress Cataloging-in-Publication Data has been applied for.

ISBN 978-0-06-279562-5

20 21 22 23 24 LSC 10 9 8 7 6 5 4 3 2

FOR THE MEN AND WOMEN WHO SERVED OUR GREAT NATION, ESPECIALLY MY BROTHERS IN ARMS WHO SACRIFICED THEIR LIVES IN THE PRESERVATION OF LIBERTY, AND FOR MY PRECIOUS WIFE, RUBY

Contents

Foreword

by Senator Bob Dole

It is often said that the true heroes of war are the ones who don't come back. In the terrible Battle of Iwo Jima, America lost 6,821 such heroes. But for the hand of God, Jack Lucas would have been one of them. During some of the most intense fighting on that sulfur island, on D day plus one, two grenades rolled into Lucas's trench. Without hesitation, the seventeen-year-old threw himself on one and pulled the second underneath his body, absorbing a deadly blast with his own flesh and bone. Though he saved the three Marines who were with him, he did much more than that. By that act Jack Lucas exemplified with his own blood and grit the spirit of sacrifice that won the war in the Pacific. All Americans should know his story; our foes should contemplate it.

Jack's life was not unlike my own. We both grew up during the Depression as middle-class kids in a small town, though my experience was spent in Kansas and his in North Carolina. When the Japanese bombed Pearl Harbor we both knew it was our destiny to answer our nation's call. I was a college freshman whose biggest concerns were planning the next fraternity party and finding a date for Saturday night. Jack, on the other hand, was still being told what time to go to bed, and his biggest plan was graduating eighth grade.

Though I knew it was inevitable I would serve, I pondered the time of my enlistment. Jack was ready to join the Marines while the bombs were still falling on Pearl Harbor. It took him almost nine months to wrangle his way past the bureaucracy that should have kept him home, entering service four months before I signed up.

While I was fighting Nazis in Italy, Jack was fighting the Japanese in the Pacific. Both of us witnessed a staggering loss of young American lives. Our own lives were forever changed by grievous personal injuries suffered in combat.

Jack and I know the horror of feeling life draining from our bodies as we lay on the field of battle, trapped in a dull haze and comforted only by morphine. We are given only one body, and when it is broken in service to others, we have given a most precious gift. Jack and I would learn to write left-handed, athletics would forever be out of the question, and our internal injuries would require a lifetime of attention. We were fortunate; at least we would have a lifetime.

Jack and I have looked over the edge into the darkness that is death and survived to tell of the ghastliness that is war. War is not glamorous. It is ugly business and no one escapes its effects. It can't be explained adequately to someone who has never been there.

Men are never closer than when they are under fire together. In World War II, we were all brothers on the battlefield. As survivors, we are left to remember those who paid the ultimate price. They too are our brothers, a relationship born in battle, baptized in blood, and immortal in spirit. We honor their memory.

From all walks of life they came, from the mountains, prairies, cities, and farms, they joined to serve. Death gave no heed to the privilege of their birth. They laid down their lives for the cause of freedom and for their buddies in the foxhole with them.

I have always felt that what gets people through a physical or emotional crisis is having a foundation of faith in God, believing that life matters and that there's a bigger plan in play than what we can see with our human eyes. In my own memoirs I wrote

> [We] need one another to defend one another, to depend on one another. They say every soldier on the front saves every other soldier's life and has his life saved by another soldier nearby.

That's the fighting man's job. Jack did his job well and, like so many that have served their country, I am proud to call him my brother.

Indestructible

Prologue

And when he gets to Heaven to St. Peter he will tell: "One more Marine reporting, Sir. I've served my time in Hell."
—Sergeant James A. Donahue, 1st Marine Division

Though I was just thirteen when I decided to march on Japan, ride the wave of American retribution, and make the Japanese pay for the attack on Pearl Harbor, I had already passed from boy to man. I thought I knew it all. Though I had yet to see friends evaporate before my eyes, or an enemy bleed out and die by my own hand, I had loved and now I had hated and I considered myself more than ready to go to war.

That I would find both the need and the strength to pull a live hand grenade to my gut while a second grenade lay beneath me, ready to detonate, would have astonished me even in my moments of greatest bravado. I went to war with vengeance in my heart. I went to war to kill. Such is the irony of fate that I will be remembered for saving the lives of three men I barely knew.

My journey into manhood began one bleak October afternoon when my beloved father drew his final breath, having lost his long battle with cancer. I was eleven years old. Afterward, I pushed away any man the lovely widow, Margaret Lucas, attempted to bring into our lives. I did not need a man; I was one. I was a tough kid who loved to fight. I was rebellious by nature and had a hair-trigger temper. Troubled in general: that was the young Jack Lucas.

As my inner turmoil heated up so did world events, and with the reprehensible bombing of Pearl Harbor, we both boiled over. I lived by my wits and often made up my own rules, leaving a trail of broken jaws and busted lips as I went along. So, it was not much of a stretch on my part when I found a way to join the United States Marine Corps, though I was only fourteen at the time. I went AWOL to catch a train headed in the direction of the war. Then I stowed away on a ship to reach one of the Pacific's worst battlefields. I figured, if I figured anything at all, that if I was shrewd enough to impose my will on the United States Marine Corps, the Japs would give me little trouble.

Having already borne the weight of my life's biggest loss, I was not afraid to face whatever awaited me on Red Beach One, Iwo Jima. I had no way of knowing that in a matter of a few short hours I would make the most important decision of my life and in the lives of three members of my fire team. The choice would be mine: either I could die alone or all of us would die together.

I was decorated with the Medal of Honor, a North Carolina farm boy catapulted to national fame. The subsequent years were mercurial, reaching heights as high as the gallery above both houses of Congress when President Bill Clinton introduced me to my nation, and as low as discovering a contract had been taken out on my life by someone who was supposed to love me.

For decades I fought the Japanese in my sleep, my arms thrashing about, shouting sharp yet incoherent words. I would never shake the images of mutilated young men or the faces of the dead and dying. The details always stayed fresh, and my horror at their numbers never faded. Though their faces would never go away, in time I would learn to accept them as friends to whom I had made a commitment in blood to honor.

I discovered that we are all a product of our own personal histories, formed by the influences of family, who likewise were formed by theirs. From my earliest memory, my parents instilled patriotism in my character. The first time a favorite uncle placed a Marine dress cover on my head at age eight, I was instantly transformed and I knew my place would be with the United States Marine Corps. Throughout my life the Corps has been a beacon to guide me and an anchor to hold me in a place where I belonged. No matter where I have hung my hat, my heart has always been with the Corps. As long as I am able, I will find the time to talk to any Marine who approaches me and though it is a struggle, thanks to those two grenades that once burst beneath me in the black ash, I will scratch out an autograph or two. I see a little of myself in every Marine. They are bright, strong, and eager to carry the torch passed from my generation to theirs. One fact has remained steadfast: I still fully appreciate my country and those gallant Americans who serve her. They are my heroes, one and all.

I turned these thoughts over in my mind earlier this year as I reached down and dug deep furrows with my fingers in Iwo Jima's warm volcanic ash. I held the black grains tightly in my palm. The substance that made up this island, 650 miles south of Japan, was composed of sulfur, rock, and ash. I had returned to this beach for the sixtieth anniversary of the deadliest battle in Marine Corps history. It was still an ugly little piece of real estate, seemingly worthless and reeking of sulfur. However, in 1945, this tiny pork chop–shaped island was quite valuable, not only to the Americans, but to the Japanese as well.

Three years into World War II the United States had no long-range fighter escorts to protect their B-29 bombers en route to Japan from American-held Saipan in the Mariana Islands, 1,500 miles south of Japan. In order for the United States to provide protection for these flights, as well as a safe landing site for the bombers that fell prey to Japanese fighters, it was essential an American-held airfield be situated on Iwo Jima. When a straight line was drawn from Saipan to Japan, it crossed the Volcano Islands at the halfway point between the two. Wresting the island away from the Japanese would not come cheaply. Before this land would become American-held, our nation would pay dearly for it in the lives of her best and brightest young men. Roughly two miles wide and four miles long, this small volcanic island, one-third the size of Manhattan, was home turf for the Japanese. In their entire history, no foreign army had ever successfully invaded Japanese territory. All that was about to change and it would change here on this island called Iwo Jima.

The Japanese dug fifteen hundred chambers into the island rock, each connected by sixteen miles of tunnels and built on as many as five different levels. The Japanese strategy was simple. Every soldier was ordered to kill ten Americans before they were themselves killed. It was not their intention to survive. These defenders of Japanese soil were prepared for the American invasion not only physically, but also mentally.

It took forty days for the fleet of more than five hundred ships carrying the 4th and 5th Marine Divisions to sail from Hawaii to Iwo Jima, with a short stopover at Saipan. The 3rd Division sailed from Guam to join them creating an armada of 880 ships, carrying 110,000 troops into battle—more Marines than ever before.

Preceding the troop invasion, Iwo Jima was ferociously pounded by the United States in the longest sustained aerial offensive and naval bombardment of the war, but it had little effect against the subterranean fortresses. Burrowed into these fortifications, lying in wait, were more than twenty thousand of the Emperor's soldiers.

Around 0900 the first wave of Marines stormed the beach. Unable to dig effective foxholes in the shifting grains of ash, the Americans were easy targets for the

Japanese. Mortars, heavy artillery, and machine gun fire crisscrossed the beaches, raining death down on the Marines and creating mass confusion. The battle that was expected to last three days would wage for a grueling thirty-six.

At an elevation of 550 feet, Mount Suribachi rises high above the landing beaches. From this volcanic cone at Iwo's southern tip, Japanese gunners covered every inch of the beach. Additional fortifications flanked the landing beaches. Japanese forces were equipped with rockets and antitank guns, all at the ready. From the moment his landing craft approached, every American was always within range of enemy guns. Dogged Marines were challenging an unseen enemy and could only meet their objective by tenacity and courage, one bloody inch at a time.

Before an American flag flew atop Mount Suribachi, America's fighting men suffered more than 6,000 casualties; by the end of the battle the death toll had reached 6,821 and there were over 19,000 wounded men. In addition, more than twenty thousand Japanese defenders lost their lives. It was the beginning of the end.

As a young man I was a voluntary and very eager player in this extraordinary episode of American history. At that time I was in top physical form and ready to fight every Japanese soldier on the island. I thought I knew everything there was to know of any importance. By the time I was carried off of Iwo Jima I had learned much more about *esprit de corps* and the sacrifices men are willing to make for each other than I could ever have imagined. Now, a lifetime later, this ol' warhorse had returned to Iwo Jima, much older and wiser. While emotions as deep as the ocean around me came flooding back, I surveyed Iwo's landscape once again and waves of memories washed over me.

1

December 7, 1941

When this war is over, the Japanese language
will be spoken only in hell.

—Admiral Bill Halsey

The first news bulletins went out over the air around
1430 Eastern Standard time, December 7, 1941. The
Sunday afternoon NBC broadcast of "Swing 'n Sway
with Sammy Kaye" was temporarily interrupted to report the shocking account of the Japanese attack on
Pearl Harbor. The announcement flashed its way from
Hawaii to every corner of the world. Stunned Americans
hovered over their radios, gleaning every available scrap
of information from the broadcasts; I was no exception.

Most Americans had never heard of Pearl Harbor, and while they may have understood little about its military significance and location, everyone was angered by the United States having been "suddenly and deliberately" attacked.

I was a thirteen-year-old cadet captain at Edwards Military Institute, in the little town of Salemburg, North Carolina, during that period. Along with other cadets, I was in the dining hall when word came of the attack around the time of the evening meal. The commandant, Alsa Gavin, entered the room and asked for everyone's attention. He made the announcement, "The Japanese have bombed Pearl Harbor, destroyed a number of our ships, and killed many of our sailors." A chill ran down my spine. Having been reared with a profound love of country, I was devastated at the thought of Americans being killed and injured by sneak attack. In an instant my life was forever changed, and from that point on, I was obsessed with the desire to kill Japanese.

I was aware of Japan's invasion of China and the atrocities that had occurred in Nanjing at its hands. I knew the Germans were sinking a lot of our transport ships carrying supplies to Great Britain and our Merchant Marines were being killed, even though we were not at war.

My fellow cadets and I quietly left our unfinished meals and went to the nearest radio for more information. There was a radio in the day room of the barracks and several of us gathered around it, anxiously anticipating every new report from Pearl Harbor. The details of the attack were sketchy, but the alarmed tone of the newscasters spoke volumes; America had been dealt a devastating blow. Men had died horrible deaths and more would follow in the aftermath of the assault. I remember fearing that there would be an invasion on American soil somewhere, though no one was talking about joining the military. Over the course of the next few days everyone was eager for America to do something.

Sunday night, just after "lights out," I lay wide-awake in my quarters. Tomorrow was another school day, but my mind was no longer on education. My thoughts were hopelessly locked on the attack. I made every effort to sleep, but it was of little use. Every time I closed my eyes, the images of Americans dying at Pearl Harbor flashed like a nickelodeon in my head.

Though I was only an eighth grader, I had the foresight to realize the Japanese were not planning to stop in the Pacific. Their goal was Main Street in every city and hamlet in America. Something powerful was pushing me, taking control of me. I did not know it at the time, but that "something" was my destiny calling. I would not settle for watching from the sidelines when the United States was in such desperate need of support from its citizens. Everyone was needed to do his part and I could not do mine by remaining in North Carolina while one of the most dramatic events in history played itself out half a world away. The cadets at Edwards were our nation's future military force. We were expected to someday take our place among America's fighting men. My "someday" was December 7, 1941.

At Edwards, we slept on metal spring beds with larger-than-usual mattresses on top. I had it better than most; I had one roommate, Bernard. Other cadets had three. There were no closets, only a wardrobe in which to store our clothing. There had been a lot of fun times shared in that room. I loved to entertain my friends by fashioning a cape out of a bath towel and leaping from the wardrobe to the bed yelling, "Look, I'm Captain Marvel!" Nothing pleased me more than to make everyone laugh. From my window I could look beyond the parade ground to the senior barracks on the other side. Prior to Sunday's attack, those barracks had been my goal. I would do well in school, be promoted to the senior barracks, and eventually graduate. I felt differently now—everything had changed. I wasn't a kid anymore. My goal was much farther away than the parade ground; it stretched thousands of miles beyond to the Pacific.

I was different than other young men my age, possessing a military aptitude and discipline well beyond my years. At Edwards I had acquired knowledge of military formations and drilling. It was a way of life I loved. However, at the age of thirteen, driven to avenge this cowardly unprovoked attack against our nation, I made the decision to join the United States Marine Corps.

Since my father was deceased, I asked Uncle Tom Lucas, my father's older brother, about joining the Marines, but he kept putting me off. I can only guess he was stalling in hopes I would change my mind. Growing impatient, I went to my mother. She was aghast at my request and refused to sign the required consent forms. As months passed, I was unable to resume my regular routine like the other cadets. They continued to study and participate in school activities. All the while, my rage against the Japanese escalated in me to such a fever pitch, I could not concentrate on anything other than how to scheme my way into the Marine Corps.

My mother instilled patriotism in me from as early as I can remember and she strongly supported the American military. However, when I confronted her a second time with the prospect of signing a consent form, she declined again. My mother told me, "I only have two children and I don't want to lose you. You are only fourteen years old and I won't let you go off to war. Maybe when you're sixteen." I repeatedly requested her signature on the consent form and she repeatedly refused it.

All Americans hated the Japanese and I was no different. The only difference between other Americans and me was the fact that most of them were doing something about it and I was not. I knew we were at war with Nazi Germany too, but as horrible as its offenses were, it had not attacked my country. The battle cry was "Remember Pearl Harbor!" and I heard it and felt it deep inside me and was restless to respond. I had no control over my desire to defend my country, nor was there a real explanation for those feelings.

America struggled militarily to find her footing and I grew more determined than ever to get in the fight. For me, fighting the Japanese was simply an extension of the values I learned as a child, to defend good against evil. The Lucas family—my kin—enjoyed a legacy of helping others and playing the sometime dangerous role of rescuer.

In 1903, my grandfather, William Lucas, had a twelve-year-old niece named Mae Phelps. Mae was the progeny of William's sister, Mollie Lucas Phelps. Mollie had died and her husband remarried. A neighbor, living across the road from Mae, informed my grandfather that his young niece was suffering at the hands of her father. Mae was not allowed to attend school. Instead, she was forced to work like a farmhand from dawn until dusk. Grandfather was furious. He, along with his son, borrowed a boat and rowed down the Roanoke River to a landing near the child's home.

The kind neighbor went to find young Mae and located her in the barn milking a cow. She was informed that her uncle, William, was waiting across the road at the neighbor's house to take her to live with him. Mae said her father was away and would be furious when he returned if she had not finished her chores. The neighbor assured her William would protect her. Dressed only in rags and taking nothing with her, she dropped everything and ran toward William, her rescuer. When my grandfather saw her condition he was enraged. Mae was terrified of what would happen when her father came home and found her gone. Wil-

liam told her she was going to live with his family and her father had no say in the matter. Through trembling lips she pleaded, "Oh, could I? Could I, please?"

Mae took a bath at the neighbor's house and was given some clothes to wear. In the meantime, Mae's father had come home and noticed her absence. Apparently his wife had witnessed the child's departure and directed him to her whereabouts. Mae's father charged across the road bellowing, threatening, and cussing with every stride. "I'm gonna' beat the hell out of you two," he yelled. William's sixteen-year-old son met the man at the edge of the road and said, "I've got a knife and I'll cut your guts out!" William came out of the neighbor's house and told Mae's father she was leaving with them, and if he knew what was good for him, he would make no attempt to come after her. Mae's father left angry, but the confrontation was over. Mae was welcomed into the Lucas home and wrapped in an abundance of love and tenderness she had not known since the death of her mother.

———

I ALWAYS ENJOYED hearing the tale of my grandfather's liberation of the young girl and very much admired his role as rescuer. My life somewhat paralleled the tragic life of my distant cousin, Mae. After the death of my father, my mother married a man from Belhaven, North Carolina, named Radford Jones. My father was a good provider and left my mother adequate funds for our care. Once Radford entered our lives, things changed. We moved from our home in Plymouth, North Carolina, to Belhaven, and my mother set him up in an automotive sales business. Radford spent the seven years he was married to my mother going through most of her money.

Radford was a sad individual. He drank too much, a habit which in years to come would cost him his life in a one-car accident. Radford's father died as a result of a self-inflicted gunshot wound. Radford's youngest son, Cliff Jones, was also an alcoholic and died before his time. Radford and I had a unique understanding. He did not like me, and likewise, I did not like him. I refused to recognize him as an authoritative figure and tensions between us often flared. He persisted in his attempts to dominate me. He simply did not understand. I took orders from no man, except my father, and he was gone. We continued to have this misunderstanding until one day when I threatened to throw him down some steps.

Radford later proved to be an ally. He was very much in favor of my joining the Marines.

Radford had two sons from a previous marriage. Cliff was near the same age as my younger brother, Louis Ed Lucas. Cliff's older brother was named Billy Jones, and everybody liked him. Billy had one of those personalities that you could not help but like, and I was no exception. He was the older brother I never had. Billy joined the navy before Pearl Harbor. I knew that he and others like him were placing themselves in harm's way because America was in trouble, and they loved her so. I loved her too and the thought of another country inflicting harm on her hurt me. The obsession to strike back continued to consume me.

My father would have never supported my decision to fight at such a young age and he would have been the only one who could have stopped me. I was too much for my mother to handle. Determined to join the Marines, I told my mother not to expect any further cooperation from me as far as school was concerned. My words were, "I will see, feel, hear, and do nothing until I am allowed to join the service. My education can be completed later. Might as well let me go." Knowing me as she did, my mother did not underestimate the measure of my resolve. She cried and told me she loved me. Against very strong objections, and because of her refusal to lie for me, I forged her signature on the necessary form and hugged her goodbye. With tears in her eyes, she embraced me and wished me well.

Radford Jones happily drove me to the recruiting station at Norfolk, Virginia. It was a quiet trip. My stepfather thought he was benefiting from the deal and I thought I was. My joining up was the only thing we ever agreed on.

With a muscular build, five feet eight inches of height, and weighing 180 pounds, I had the appearance of someone well beyond my years when I walked through the front door and took my place at the end of the line. It was not long before I heard the recruiter snap, "Next!" I took a deep breath and approached his desk. He looked me over carefully. Attempting to project a semblance of maturity, I was quick and sure with my responses, giving all the right answers. The recruiter asked, "Where's your birth certificate?" I replied, "I didn't think I'd need one as long as I had my mother's signature on the consent form." Radford Jones, anxious to eradicate me from his life, was swift to explain that he was my stepfather and I was indeed seventeen. He sold me to the Marine Corps with all the skill of a car salesman. I am not sure the recruiter was totally convinced, but the military needed warm bodies and I met that requirement. With an affirmative nod, he directed me toward a line of recently accepted recruits. I exhaled a long sigh of relief.

I looked around and Radford was nowhere to be seen. As soon as he was sure he was rid of me, he left. I sat on a bench with the other guys and rested the back of my head against the cool gray-green plaster wall behind me. There was little conversation between me and the other recruits. It was important to keep my business to myself and not give anything away. I sat there, thoroughly pleased with my triumph, and could not help but smile at the prospect of the wonderful adventures that lay ahead.

Deep in thought, it occurred to me that I was following in the footsteps of countless Americans who, throughout history, were compelled to fight for their country. Some left mighty big shoes to fill and I hoped my feet could fill them. Two centuries ago, my forefathers took up arms against the oppressive King George III. A century later, my great-grandfather defended our homeland against an aggressive North. A miniball wounded him in the right frontal bone on a battlefield in Virginia. After four months of convalescence, he returned to the line. His father, at age fifty-four, enlisted as a private in the Confederacy. Sadly, he died from malaria while proudly serving his homeland. Both my mother's and my father's families were Irish, and I was a descendant of no less than two recipients of the Victoria's Cross, the British government's highest award for valor.

I was prepared to join the ranks in the same spirit that had prompted men to answer their country's call for centuries. At the age of fourteen, after proudly swearing to defend my country, I became a United States Marine. Sitting there in the Norfolk recruiting station, I was just a face in the crowd. No one could have suspected events had been set in motion that would ultimately include the Medal of Honor.

2

The Making of a Warrior

There is nothing so likely to produce peace as
to be well prepared to meet the enemy.

      —President George Washington

In 1715, an Englishman named Colonel Al-
exander Parris purchased an island in South
Carolina. It was a flourishing plantation up
until the Civil War. The first Marines were
stationed there in 1891 in the form of a small
security detachment. The island was officially
designated a recruiting depot on November
1, 1915, and the Marines never left. During

the fateful December of 1941, 5,272 recruits arrived at Parris Island, South Carolina. The following month, they were joined by 9,206 of their brothers, making it necessary to increase the number of Recruit Training Battalions from four to twelve. At its peak, during the summer of 1942, as many as one thousand trainees crowded Parris Island's rifle range each week. On December 5, 1942, President Franklin Roosevelt, by executive order, halted the voluntary enlistment of individuals subject to the draft, thereby forcing the Marine Corps to meet its personnel requirements through the Selective Service.

LIKE OTHER NEW enlistees, I was transported from Norfolk, Virginia, to a little rail station in Yemassee, South Carolina, not far from Parris Island. The train that carried me was an old-style steam locomotive, with a rope strung through the center of the cars so the conductor could signal the engineer when he wanted the train to stop. From Yemassee, trucks hauled us under cover of darkness to Parris Island. It was a regular practice to bring new recruits into camp in this manner in order to prevent their knowledge of an escape route. As we stepped off the truck, I looked around at my new surroundings. I heard the drill sergeant bark, "Give your heart to Jesus boys, 'cause your butt now belongs to me!" We were issued clothing and sea bags before being marched to Quonset huts about one quarter of a mile away. Each hut slept sixteen men. We were promptly assigned bunks and sacked out for the night.

The sergeant ordered, "Lights out!" At approximately the same time, lights were going out on the cadets at Edwards Military Institute back in North Carolina. They would wake in the morning and prepare to become future military men, but not me; with the rising sun, I would be doing it for real. The voices around me began to hush, down to a few whispers at first, trailing into random sounds of restlessness, and finally, silence filled the room. I plumped my pillow and adjusted my blanket in an attempt to get comfortable on the upper GI bunk. All around me the hut was immersed in total darkness, but for the intense glow of satisfaction shining brightly on my face.

The day after my enlistment, August 7, 1942, the 1st Marine Division landed on Guadalcanal in the first major Allied offensive in the war in the Pacific. The hot humid climate supported malaria and disease-carrying mosquitoes, and posed a continuous threat of fungal infections and fever. Enduring rats, insects, and drenching rains, it took the Marines three months to establish a beachhead and secure the airfield. The Allies had begun taking back the region and there was great jubilation among us that our offensive action had begun in the Pacific. I was impatient to be a part of it.

"Fall out, now! You've got five minutes to get outta' here. Turn loose your cot and grab your socks." The bugler played a reveille. We fell in and proceeded to the mess hall. Following the blessing of the meal, we all stabbed a steak on a platter in the middle of the table. If you were slow, you got left out. This was our first lesson in quickness and survival training.

Drill instructors interrogated us about our experience and I indicated my military school training. This disclosure put me in a position where I assisted in the drilling of recruits. "To the rear, march! To the rear, march!" At each command these fledgling Marines failed to perform even the simplest of drills. Men clumsily stumbled and bumped into each other. Marching first in one direction and then another, they looked more like Keystone Cops from Hollywood's silent film era than soldiers. What a pitiful sight they were. Across the field, the drill instructor watched me perform my duties from the cool shade of

a large oak tree. I was tough and executed my responsibilities well. The instructor and the recruits respected me
for it. One can only imagine what their thoughts would
have been had they known they were being instructed by
a fourteen-year-old boy.

I was in my element, performing the duty for which
I was predestined. As long as I could remember, I had
always wanted to be a Marine. When I was about nine,
my uncle, John Frank Edwards, gave me a Marine dress
hat, or "dress cover," as the Marines call it. The hat was
styled with a leather visor. I cherished it. I felt different
when I placed it upon my head. When I wore it on the
school bus, bigger boys would take it away from me, toss
it around, and then pull my coattails over my head. I
fought them until they tired of me. Possession of that cap
planted the pride of the Corps in me very early in life.

The whole theme of Marine Corps training is to cre-
ate warriors. Basic training was rough and Parris Island
lived up to its reputation of toughness, discipline, and
thoroughness. The enforcing of these three factors is
what makes Marines the best-trained fighting force in
the world. Calisthenics, long marches, and drilling were
performed in the hot August sun until someone passed
out. That was a lesson in building stamina, and stamina
would be needed when we hit the beaches.

There was constant cursing and abuse from instructors and they had a tendency to use offensive language. As if questioning our parentage was not painful enough, the men would occasionally strike recruits that did not perform to their expectations. Sometimes they inflicted serious injuries. Once, a sergeant slammed a helmet on my head so hard, blood trickled down my nose. I blocked out the pain and never let it bother me. Not every recruit was Marine material.

In addition to hard knocks received from instructors, some Marines faced assault from fellow Marines. We had one in our outfit who refused to bathe. I do not know how he could stand his own filth; I know we could not stand him. One day we jumped him and remedied the problem in short order.

Parris Island gave extensive training on the rifle range, and once our rifle training began, we camped at the range. During this period, I learned a lesson that would prove invaluable during my career as a Marine. A drill instructor asked for a volunteer to drive a truck. I was quick to offer my services and was promptly issued a wheelbarrow with which to dispense ammunition along the firing line. In the future, I would never volunteer for anything.

There was great jubilation upon graduating basic. We

were now full-fledged Marines, having completed our first training hurdle. We had received a lot more than physical training and discipline; our spirits, as well, were forever changed. A bond had developed between us—a bond that would last a lifetime. We belonged to the world's premier fighting force, an organization older than the country it served. To complete basic was to accomplish immortality. Anyone who was ever a Marine, even if he served in different wars, continues to live on in the Marines newly claiming the "Title." Marines are men and women of character who have a deep love of country and the Corps, but more importantly, for each other.

My next assignment was Jacksonville Naval Air Station in Florida. Before I returned to Yemassee to catch the southbound train to my new base, my buddies took me to the liquor store. They asked me what I wanted to drink. I had no idea what to request, and hesitated just long enough for someone to suggest corn liquor. That sounded good to me and I got a pint. It tasted nothing like the scuppernong wine we had during the holidays back home. I overdid it a little, and by the time I woke up, I was in Florida. It was October 2, 1942. By comparison, Jacksonville was a definite improvement over Parris Island. There were no Quonset huts and the camp had concrete barracks, much nicer than those to which we were accustomed.

The nearby Roosevelt Hotel was a favorite to Marines on liberty. It had a first-rate bar and dining room. I saw a very attractive girl there one night and we started talking. She was from North Carolina and I became very interested in her. I spent half the money I had with me on a little bracelet for her. When the evening grew late, I walked her home and kissed her goodnight at her door. Her pretty face and shape remained fixed in my mind long after the evening ended. I could not wait until I got another opportunity to see her. When liberty rolled around again, I headed straight for the Roosevelt Hotel. I scanned the room anxiously. I spied her in the center of the lobby with some guy in a tuxedo. A mink coat was casually draped around her shoulders. Another lesson learned; I must acquire great wealth to get the "uptown ladies."

My stay in Jacksonville was brief and I was soon transferred thirty miles farther south to the Naval Air Station at Green Cove Springs on December 31, 1942. We got tougher while in Green Cove. I was assigned gate guard duty and given a shotgun and a jeep. The jeep had a manual transmission. I loved to change gears and patrol the camp perimeter. Could life get any better?

At Green Cove I went on liberty, drank with the guys, and visited dance clubs. Eighteen- and nineteen-year-old women would drag me out on the dance floor and we would swing to the rhythm of various Glenn Miller tunes. During those years, one of my favorite songs was "Rum and Coca-Cola" by the Andrews Sisters. *Native girls all dance and smile. Help soldier celebrate his leave. Make everyday like New Year's Eve.* It had some pretty racy lyrics for that time. At the age of fourteen, I did not possess the finesse on the dance floor that I would acquire later on, but I got by. I developed my own modified style of jitterbugging and became a popular dance partner. There was not much I would rather do than dance, but that had not always been the case.

I was only ten years old when my mom dressed me in a white linen suit and sent me off to my first dance. It was not much of a dance; the girls chased the boys around the room, in an effort to get them to participate, but we ran away. The boys ended up wrestling in the grass and getting ugly green stains all over our nice clean clothes. There was a pretty girl named Martha with whom I really wanted to dance, but I was too shy to ask her. I chose instead to simply admire her from a distance. She never had any idea how much she meant to me.

I named my favorite mule Martha, after that unrequited love. Martha the mule was a handful. You never knew what she was going to do next. I could return from the field on Martha's back, and inevitably, something eventful would happen. Once, a car passed us on the road. Everything would have been fine, had the car's horn not sounded. Martha slammed on the brakes, throwing me over her head and onto the ground. I lay on the dirt road, still holding on to the reins and looking up at Martha's simple expression.

She was ornery, stubborn, and headstrong. Those were her good points. One duty Martha hated more than any other was pulling the hay wagon to the field. I would hook up her harness, climb aboard, and cross my fingers. I knew it was only a matter of time before it happened; it always did. As soon as she realized the wagon was attached to her, she began to let the biggest, foulest, and loudest of farts. After a couple of good backfires, she started splattering and spewing the worst imaginable mess of muck in my general direction. It was the same story, every time.

I was always a creative sort of kid, and not wanting the beast to get the best of me, I came up with a solution. I swept out the hay wagon and laid the broom against the side panel. Ever so gently, I fastened Martha's yolk to the wagon. She eyeballed me once or twice, but I quickly soothed her spirit with a firm pat and a softly spoken, "Whoa, Martha. Good girl."

I climbed into the wagon, took the reins, and gripped tightly. Firmly, but calmly, I uttered, "Giddyap mule." From where I was sitting, I thought I heard a faint rumble. It sounded like a distant thunderstorm approaching, the kind you get late in the afternoon on a warm summer day. I examined the sky and all appeared clear. If there was to be a storm, it was still far enough away for me to load some hay before it rained. Once again, I signaled, "Giddyap mule!"

Martha's tail twitched and slowly arched upward. Her tail rose and my eyes widened, as the realization of impending attack loomed large. I determined from her stance, and the resonance of her thundering intestines, the need to brace myself. I reached for the broom and poised the weapon in "javelin throw" position. The instant I had a clear shot, I thrust my weapon forward, ramming the broom handle directly into the offending orifice.

I had never heard anything quite like the sound that bellowed forth from Martha. Her high-pitched screeching was reminiscent of an emergency vehicle's siren. Martha most assuredly had an emergency, and it was stuck right in the south end of the northbound mule.

She bucked and reared, kicking loose the wagon's floorboards. Martha broke into a run, giving me a wild ride all around the yard. At the first opportunity, I jumped from the wagon and made good my escape. I can only imagine what poor Martha envisioned in her pint-size mule brain. She must have thought the dreaded wagon had been driven right up her rear.

The broomstick became dislodged in all the fury and Martha stopped. She looked back at the wagon and shook slightly at the withers. My mother came running into the yard and asked,

"What's got into that mule?" I shrugged and responded, "Bumblebee, I think."

I WAS NOT scared of girls anymore. These small, tender creatures were soft, warm, and smelled really nice. Women were very affectionate, some more than others. One of my favorites was a woman named Betty, a beautiful waitress living in Palatka, Florida. I walked in a café one day and started talking to her. I liked the sweet way she spoke to me. Almost immediately, we made plans for our first date which took place that very evening.

We double-dated with another Marine and his girl. Betty drove her father's car and I rode up front with her. At one point during the evening she found a nice place for us to park. While the other Marine and his girl were busy entertaining each other, Betty made her move on me. She expressed concern that the November evening was chilly. "May I warm your hands?" she asked. What could I say? Betty took my hand in hers and slowly guided it under her blouse. She was sitting on my lap. I was utterly defenseless, an adolescent victim of this older, more experienced woman. She must have been all of nineteen. I began to feel warm and weak all over. While it was

wonderful and exciting, the experience was also star-
tling. Part of me was ready to face death in battle, while
another part was poised to experience a woman's love. I
think the latter worried me the most.

Two days later, Betty and I ventured out once more.
Unlike before, we were alone on this occasion. She drove
us to a beautiful spot overlooking the Palatka River.
Cooler weather had created a crystal clear night. The atmosphere alone was positively intoxicating. By the light
of a full Florida moon, I experienced another previously
unexplored area of the grownup world. Betty invited
me to follow her into the backseat. Utterly powerless
against such skill, this helpless Marine succumbed to her
charms. To my credit, she had no clue about the degree
of my youth and inexperience. The evening was great. I
had very little knowledge of romance and Betty was my
first big conquest, unless you count that little incident
with my neighbor-friend when I was thirteen.

*I loved anything to do with the sport of box-
ing: magazines, pictures, posters, and newspaper articles. It was a favorite hobby of mine. I
kept a collection of memorabilia in my room.
Down the street lived a girl, a year younger
than me, who frequently came by my house*

to visit. One day we were home alone and I wanted to share my hobby with her. I cannot remember the details of what happened next, only that we were not alone in my room very long before one thing led to another, and I was showing her a lot more than my boxers. The session ended almost as quickly as it began. She had taught me a lesson I would never forget: offering to show a girl your boxers can lead to a whole new favorite hobby.

DURING THIS PERIOD of time, while I was still learning to be a soldier and a man, other American men were putting themselves on the line all over the world. My stepbrother, Billy, was one of those brave heroes. Billy was a fireman first class, serving aboard DD430, the USS *Eberle*. The *Eberle* set sail for South Atlantic patrol the day after Christmas, 1942. On March 10, 1943, she intercepted the Karin, a German blockade runner. Fourteen of the *Eberle*'s crew boarded the Karin, including Billy. Demolition charges set by the enemy exploded, instantly killing Billy and six of his fellow crewmen. His body was never recovered. He received the Silver Star and Purple Heart for his actions; they were sent to his mother. It must have seemed a poor exchange for a parent to open a box containing a piece of metal in exchange for a son. I craved the opportunity to fight our nation's enemies. Losing Billy heightened that desire even more.

On June 22, 1943, the Marine Corps assigned me to Camp Geiger, North Carolina, a small base in close proximity to Camp Lejuene. Marines assembled at Camp Geiger from other camps to receive machine gun training. I excelled in the various aspects of Marine training. However, I was young and occasionally acted foolish to let off a little steam.

One day, a bunch of us went to the head. There were windows over the "pee trough" and we challenged each other to break out the glass panes with our fists. After shattering the first two, we found the third would not break. I gave it a good punch. My fist made contact at an awkward angle and shards of glass were driven deep into the flesh of my hand, cutting all the way to the bone. My buddies took me to a corpsman to treat the injury. As I bit down on a stack of tongue depressors, he performed the profoundly painful procedure of removing each sliver of glass. Every day it seemed I learned something new.

During warm weather, I took a couple of my buddies home to Belhaven, North Carolina, for a weekend visit.

My mother fixed us all a good home-cooked meal. After supper, we went down to the local drug store, hung out at the soda fountain, and saw some friends. I took my fellow Marines to the beach; it was only a block from the house. Young people were stretched out in the sun, enjoying the warm ocean breeze. We all just kicked back, enjoying being lazy for a while. I watched a kid heading for the docks with his cane pole and a can of freshly dug worms. He reminded me of when I was a kid, which had not been so long before. As a child, I would come down to the docks with a string, a twenty-penny nail, and a piece of chicken. I would drop it into the water, tie the string around my finger, pull my straw hat down over my eyes, and wait. Eventually, a hungry crab would grab the bait and start taking it out to sea. I would pull in my catch and take it home to my mother. She made the best crab cakes in town.

The visit to Belhaven ended all too soon and the guys and I boarded a bus at the local station for the ride back to Camp Geiger. That was my last trip home as an obscure hometown boy. When I would next return, I will have been catapulted to fame and hailed as a national hero.

Training on water-cooled machine guns, we learned about first gunner and second gunner duties at Camp

Geiger. I was a first gunner. It was my job to carry the tripod on my back to the location the weapon was to be assembled. The second gunner's job was to set the gun on the tripod and load the ammunition. Finally, the first gunner would take over as the "trigger man." We learned to set up fields of fire for different situations and types of terrain to establish effective support for frontline troops.

I finished at the top of my class and qualified for heavy machine gun operation on August 20, 1943. On September 21, a private delivered an envelope containing my orders. I received my new assignment. I was to remain at Camp Geiger, along with nine others, to relieve the senior cadre of instructors who were shipping out toward the hostilities. I could not have imagined a greater disappointment. Why would the Marines hold a fighter like me behind? I knew I would make a fine instructor, but I felt my talents would be better used in real combat. I did not join the Marines to train others. I joined to kill the enemy myself.

I had learned a long time before that if you want to keep a secret, you don't tell anybody. I kept my orders, as well as my decision not to follow them, to myself. When the time finally arrived for the others in my outfit to pack up and head west, I packed my own sea bag and quietly joined them. None of them had any idea I was supposed to remain at Camp Geiger, nor did I tell them. I didn't have a worry in the world about what I was doing. What were they going to do to me if I got caught? Put me in the brig? The maximum time I would have received was thirty days, so I did not care if they did incarcerate me. I would have gone when I was released; I was hell-bent to go to war.

It was mid-December, and though winter was officially two days away, North Carolina was firmly in its first bitter grip of the season. Along with the rest of the Marines, I threw my bag over my shoulder and headed for the station. I shuddered as the moist North Carolina chill bit through my clothing. When the warm air from our lungs came in contact with the crisp atmosphere, little puffs of vapor emerged from our mouths. We looked like a line of fierce fire-breathing Marines. As my anticipation increased, so did the frequency of vapor emissions. It made me look like the most ferocious of the bunch. I was.

The train had a center aisle with bench seats facing each other. I found myself a place to sit, put my feet up on the seat across from me, and settled in. Eventually, the coal burner shuddered and lurched forward. As the locomotive's wheels began turning, I pitched my head forward and back, as if trying to make them go faster. With their every revolution I was getting closer and closer to the war. It thrilled me to be under way. I was a United States Marine headed for war in the vast Pacific. It was but a technicality that I was going AWOL in order to do it.

3

Reflections

We are still masters of our fate. We are still captain of our souls.

—Winston Churchill

My body swayed gently as the train rumbled its way
cross-country. At some point I happened to focus on my
shoes. They rocked back and forth on their heels, match-
ing the rhythm of the train. They reminded me of my father's shoes. The ache that twisted my gut when I thought
about how much I missed him always rested just beneath
the surface. Had my father lived, I probably would have
been like other young boys in North Carolina, growing
up on our farm and taking life's steps at a much slower

pace. I cannot be sure what I would have been doing at that particular time if I had had a father, but I doubt I would have been headed west on a troop train filled with determination to fight the Japanese.

My father was with me in a way. He had prepared me well, having taken pains to teach me responsibility and self-sufficiency. Life on a farm was difficult, but it taught me to be dependable and it instilled an understanding of duty in my character. I worked hard plowing and caring for the livestock. Whenever a sow had a new litter, my father assigned me to care for the runt. The smallest and weakest ones needed special attention in order to grow strong and healthy. Every lesson I learned on the farm, every lesson that was handed down to me by my father, played a part in my preparation as a Marine. I was painfully aware there would be no more such lessons. I kept the ones I had very close to my heart.

Where would these feet take me now, and how would my father's lessons guide them? In the foggy twilight between awake and asleep, my mind revisited a childhood that had long since ended yet was never entirely out of reach.

My grandfather, William, was a farmer and a generous man by nature, and was well loved by his family and neighbors. He was also a good provider, a trait he handed down to his children. Around the turn of the twentieth century, he moved his ever-growing family onto a large farm named "Springwood." The grand two-story, nine-room farmhouse, once used as a hospital during the Civil War, had fallen into disrepair. Windows, walls, and woodwork were carefully restored. However, the floor—hopelessly blood-stained from the war years—was covered with handwoven carpets. As a reminder of the land's former glory, crepe myrtle flourished throughout the grounds. My grandparents saw its potential and created a wonderful home for their family.

The farm was a huge operation, meeting every imaginable need of a large family. My grandfather had a dairy, a smokehouse full of meat, fresh fruit from his own orchard, and vegetables from his garden. There was goose down for beds, comforters, and pillows. My grandmother sewed all the family's clothes and knitted with hand-spun thread. It was a good life, with family gatherings held under the oldest pecan tree in North Carolina, where favor-

ite recipes were prepared and served by loving hands. Instead of following in his father's footsteps, my father, Louis Harold Lucas, chose to learn the dairy business from his brother, William. He worked in Durham, North Carolina, for a few years before accepting a business proposition to return to the North Carolina coast and help start Maola Ice Cream Company in the little town of Washington. The business thrived.

MY FATHER MET and fell in love with a petite honey-blonde named Margaret Edwards. They married in 1924. In 1928, I arrived on the one day of the year designated for love—February 14. It must have been a curse, because nothing has gotten me in more trouble in my life than my pursuit of love. That same year my grandfather became very ill and needed help managing the family business. Under the circumstances, my father left the dairy operation, got a home in Plymouth, and took on the responsibility of the family farm. Six months later, my grandfather passed away. My father, feeling pushed out of the family business by others and wanting a farm of his own, decided it was time to move along. I was five when my father bought a tobacco farm a few miles from Plymouth and we relocated to a comfortable white farmhouse. During the Depression we had a full smokehouse, a bountiful garden, and a cash crop of tobacco. We knew we were fortunate.

It was in this setting that I grew up surrounded by a loving family demonstrative of their affection towards each other. Hugs and spoken terms of endearment were part of our daily routine. We all had our duties and worked hard, but there was also time for fun. Only a short drive from Plymouth, Albemarle Sound Beach was a favorite recreational spot. It was a place we visited for rest and relaxation. However, it is not always with fondness that I think of Albemarle Sound Beach, for it was on that beach my father did something that spurred an unforunate cycle of events. Endeavoring to break up a fight between two friends, he injured his foot in the fray, and not long after, developed a severe bruise. Later, because of the development of bone spurs, the same foot required surgery. Eventually, cancer was discovered in the limb and his right leg was removed just below the knee. That was an anguished period for all the family. He was fitted with a prosthesis, but unable to farm again. I was eight or nine at the time. Following my father's surgery, I thought everything would be all right. I thought wrong.

ONLY SIX FEET above sea level and fifty miles from the first white settlement at Manteo, North Carolina, Plymouth was established well before the American Revolution. Plymouth was exactly the kind of place described as being in the "boonies." The population was such that everyone knew each other by name and profession. One well-known resident was Dr. Claudius McGowan. He had brought me into the world in 1928. Dr. McGowan began visiting our house every day. He would remove a huge syringe from his bag, insert it into my father's chest cavity, and extract large quantities of pus. Nobody would tell me anything about his condition, but they did not need to. I knew he was in bad shape.

I was fortunate to have my father at all. When I was about four years old, my father had attempted to scare away some blackbirds that were eating seed he had planted. He grabbed his shotgun and ran toward the field. Unfortunately, he lost his footing negotiating a ditch and fell. The gun discharged, shooting his hat off his head and spraying his face with powder. His vision was poor following the accident and his pupils were not properly aligned, creating the impression that he was not looking directly at the person he was talking to.

My little brother, Louis Ed, like most young kids,

often spent his days playing with other neighborhood children. Such was the case one October afternoon as I entered our house from school. As soon as my father realized I was home, he called me to his bedside. He quietly uttered the words, "Go get Louis Ed, and hurry." I ran out of the house and covered the hundred yards to our neighbor's as fast as my feet could carry me. I grabbed Louis Ed by the hand and told him he had to go home. Not wanting to leave, he cried and fought me. I dragged him all the way. I was gone less than ten minutes.

My mother's sobs could be heard as I came through the door. She was lying on a bed in an adjoining room, attended by friends. Loosening my hold on my brother, I turned my attention toward my father. Something was terribly wrong. As I approached where he lay, I knew. I dove toward his motionless body, threw my arms around his neck, and feeling all the agony a body could stand, I cried and held him as tightly as I could. From somewhere in the confusion that surrounded me, a voice whispered the obvious: my father was gone. Not wanting to let go, I clung tightly, trying to hold on to every remaining moment. I made a conscious memory of the way he felt in my arms. I would never forget the shape of his shoulders, the smell of his shaving soap, nor the texture of his hair. As someone began to tenderly pull me away, I fought them still holding tightly to my father. They pulled harder and my grip slid down his arm until I grasped my father's hand with both of mine. I desperately held on as long as I could until I was finally wrested away. It was October 12, 1939. I was eleven years old.

My father's oldest brother, Richard Lucas, was a preacher and blind for as long as I can remember. He bore the responsibility of the funeral service. Uncle Richard stood by as I raised my little brother up in my arms so he could see into the casket and pay our last respects. Louis Ed was only four years old at the time and he did not feel the pain I felt. Joy can be shared, but grief is endured alone. There would be joy in my future, but for the rest of my life I would bear the grief of the loss of my father alone.

I sat quietly on a pew with my mother. Caught in the grip of immeasurable grief, I remember little of the event. With bowed head and eyes fixed on the floor, I remained lost in my own personal thoughts. Gradually, a steady stream of tears began to roll down each cheek to the tip of my nose, until the weight was such that, one after another, huge collective droplets crashed to the floor, creating an ever-expanding pool at my feet.

I returned home and spent a great deal of time thinking about my father, trying to recall his voice, and hoping I would never forget what it sounded like when he spoke my name. With my shirttail hanging out and tie draped loosely around my neck, I sat quietly on the edge of his bed, absorbing the events of the day. That is when I noticed them—my father's shoes. They had been neatly placed by his bed, just as though he had prepared to slip his feet into them once more. I stared at them for the longest time and it occurred to me that he would never fill those shoes again. I would never hear his heavy steps or the unsteady rhythm of his gait. The sound of his soles in motion and loose floorboards squeaking under his weight was forever silenced. I remember how much that hurt and how very much I loved him.

4

Jack the Giant-Killer

Efforts and courage are not enough without
purpose and direction.

—President John F. Kennedy

The train jerked suddenly, awakening me. It came to
a stop in a quaint Texas town, whose name is lost to
me. We disembarked for a few minutes to stretch our
legs while the train was replenished with water. I leaned
against the wall of the depot and helped myself to a cola
and candy bar. Texas had some of the flattest land I had
ever seen—flat and dusty. Some other Marines joined
me for a snack and fresh air. I overheard them talking
about how great their girls back home were. One guy

complained about what a hardship it was on all his girl-
friends for him to be away. We all laughed with him. I
did not join the conversation; I had not had many girl-
friends to speak of yet. That would soon change.

The train's destination was Linda Vista, California. I
was stationed nearby at Camp Elliott, a tent city hous-
ing Marines waiting transfer to action in the Pacific.
South of Linda Vista was San Diego, and beyond that,
Tijuana. Upon arrival in California, I fell in formation
as the roll was called. Of course, my name was not on it.
When the first sergeant asked if anyone's name was not
called, I responded, "You didn't call my name, sir." He
asked why my name was not on the list. With a puzzled
expression, I responded, "Keeping up with the names
is the military's responsibility. I'm just a private; you're
the sergeant." After perusing the list he conferred with
a lieutenant. Following some discussion, my name was
simply added to the roster and my former post notified that I was now in California. It was the first time I
had assigned myself to my choice of duty in the Marine
Corps. It would not be the last.

More training awaited us at Linda Vista. They
marched us all over those California hills. I will never
understand the military; it is run like a government project. Why do they always put the tall guys in front and the

short guys in back? The short guys have to march twice as fast just to keep up.

I took my mother's .38 caliber revolver with me to California for luck. If I was truly lucky, I would not need it. One day I was in my tent, twirling the revolver around my finger in a demonstration of my flair at gunmanship. Inadvertently, a round was squeezed off. All the guys hit the ground. The projectile tore out of my tent, into the tent next door, finally embedding itself in my neighbor's wooden floor. Ammunition for the weapon was not available in combat and I ultimately shipped it home to my mother for safekeeping.

With each passing day, I was becoming a greater part of the Corps, and likewise, the Corps was becoming a greater part of me. I loved the Marines and wanted everything that went along with being one. I had completed basic training and machine gun school, and experienced the dance halls and female companionship. The only thing I had not yet obtained on my journey was a tattoo. I did not feel complete without one, and that is exactly what I got when I walked into a tattoo parlor in San Diego. I took a buddy with me, a nice guy from Pittsburgh, Pennsylvania. He chose the same tattoo as I, the Marine Corps emblem.

The basic design of the emblem dates back to 1868.

It is a symbolic representation which Americans, both civilian and military, immediately identify as "Marine." Prior to 1868, the Marines wore a variety of emblems based on the spread eagle and fouled anchor. In 1868, the seventh commandant, General Jacob Zeilin, decided on a more uniform, distinctive emblem centered on the globe.

There are three basic elements of the Marine Corps emblem: First, the anchor symbolizes the close ties of the Marine Corps with the United States Navy. Second, the globe symbolizes the "global involvement" of the United States Marine Corps. Finally, the eagle, with its wings spread full, identifies the Marine Corps with the United States. Clutched in its beak is a banner bearing the Marine Corps motto, *Semper Fidelis*, Latin for "always faithful." Marines say *"Semper Fi"* when they leave a gathering of other Marines. It is kind of like saying, "If you need any help, I'll be there for you." There is no closer brotherhood than the United States Marine Corps.

The tattoo I chose was slightly modified. My design replaced the traditional globe with the head of a bulldog. I sported it proudly on my right bicep. I looked tough and was tough, and I developed a reputation as such. My buddies called me names like "Block of Granite," and "Jack the Giant-Killer." Nobody liked a good fight better than I. Though I was never the type to start a fight, I would never walk away from one either, a lesson my father taught me about toughness early in life. He used to get down on his knees and box with me. I learned how to fight that way. He told me he had better never find out I had walked away from a fight. There was no danger in that because I never did.

Liberty is just what it sounds like: "freedom"—the freedom to go to town and have some fun. I enjoyed going on liberty. On one occasion, my two buddies and I were walking down a street in San Diego. We were happy, laughing and calling a cadence, and generally enjoying a few hours of freedom. Another group of Marines spotted us and called out, "Hey, recruits!" The comment came across as offensive, since we had probably been in the service longer than they. We all came to a stop in front of a used car lot. A chain had been strung around the establishment about waist-high to discourage anyone from removing cars from the lot. The cockiest of the bunch of interlopers singled me out, probably because I was the shortest. He boldly swaggered up to me, reached out, and flipped my tie up in my face. Though my blood pressure skyrocketed, I stood fast. At the time, I was wearing a type of hat shaped like a canoe, referred to by some servicemen as a "piss cutter." The Marine grabbed my hat, turned it sideways on my head, and with all the sarcasm he could muster, called me "Napoleon."

It irritated me that he picked a fight with a fellow Marine and that he broke up the good time we were having. Rage steamed between my ears like a boiler, shot through my right bicep, and exploded from my clinched fist. My right hook, a move years of boxing had perfected, came in contact with his left jaw like a thunderbolt. He fell backward over the chain barricade. Concerned that we may be spotted by MPs, my buddies took off and so did his. I bent down and retrieved my hat which had fallen onto the unconscious Marine. He was out like a light and wearing a stupid grin on his face. Across the street, a sailor yelled something to me and I asked him if he wanted some of the same; he did not.

I thought it dishonorable to fight a fellow Marine, but I was never one to accept abuse. I rewarded myself with refreshment from a café down the street. Since my friends had deserted me, I ate alone. A few minutes later, I noticed the brash Marine walking past the café window, holding his jaw with both hands. I know it hurt.

Most Marines went to Tijuana on liberty. Tijuana is just below the border in Mexico, and every military man had heard about *la vida loca* in Tijuana. The time had arrived for me to see it for myself. Barely fifteen, I went there on liberty. Another Marine and I started talking with two girls in a club. We did the usual and a little of the unusual. Just after dark and without any explanation whatsoever, the other Marine's girlfriend led me by the hand from the club. She smiled and giggled at me and I smiled back. We went out into the street. I may have been somewhat naive about her intentions, but it made no real difference, so I followed along. We jumped into the backseat of her car and pulled the door closed behind us. Right there, on the main street of Tijuana, she helped herself to what little remained of my innocence. People were all around, walking up and down the street, passing by the vehicle's windows. Nobody gave us a second thought; after all, this was Tijuana. We stepped from the vehicle, adjusted our clothing, and laughed at each other. Nothing like this ever happened to me back home.

After rejoining our friends in the club, and explaining our absence as a need to "go smoke," we all headed back to the border. I do not remember how I got to Tijuana or whose car I returned in, but I will never forget what happened there. Our female companions wanted to smuggle alcohol into the United States. They hid the bottles under their skirts and more under the backseat. The border guard asked us if we had anything to declare. I laughed out loud and howled, "I declare we had a good time!"

5

Yes, Colonel, I Am Only Fifteen

Liberty has never come from the government.
Liberty has always come from the subjects of it.
—President Woodrow Wilson

On November 4, 1941, less than one month before the attack on Pearl Harbor, the 2nd Engineer Battalion was relocated to Marine Barracks Navy Yard, Pearl Harbor, Hawaii. Its assignment was to construct Camp Catlin.

Exactly two years later, I set sail from San Diego to Pearl Harbor aboard the USS *Typhoon*, and arrived on November 11, 1943. I was assigned to Camp Catlin, Oahu, Hawaii. Being stationed overseas increased my salary from twenty-one to fifty-four dollars a month.

Camp Catlin functioned as a troop replacement and refurbishing depot, not my first choice of duty. I wanted to fight and felt my decision to do so was the right one. In those fateful early morning hours on December 7, 1941, as most Americans were preparing for a day of worship, our peaceful nation was subjected to an act of cowardice as never before seen. We had been sucker-punched by the Empire of Japan. To me, it was a "call to arms." I could never fully understand why my feelings were so intense. *Why* was of little importance; the fact that the desire was alive and raging inside me was all that mattered. To defend my country was an extension of the values I had always held dear, even as a child.

One day at Edwards Military Institute, a group of students were marching in formation. A group leader began walking on the heels of another cadet who was out of step. I never did like being harassed or seeing anyone else harassed. Leaders are supposed to demonstrate what is proper by example, not abuse. Having developed a sense of responsibility for others, I immediately took control of the situation. As I approached the aggressor, all eyes were upon me. I was big for my age, and few ever opted

*to mess with me. I looked the group leader in
the eye with my best "I mean business" glare,
and told him to back off.*

I DID NOT see Commandant Alsa Gavin, but he was
there somewhere. He later told me he had witnessed my
action that day. He explained that my display of leader-
ship was one of the reasons I had been selected to serve
as cadet captain. Perhaps Mr. Gavin understood me. He
was the oldest of seven children and, after his father's
health failed, he bore the brunt of the responsibility for
his family. Maybe he saw my pain because he knew it all
too well himself.

I came from tough stock. If I inherited the propensity
to fight from my father, perhaps I inherited the role of
protector from my mother.

*After the loss of my father, my family had a
sharecropper living on our farm. The sharecropper was an abusive man, who often mis-
treated his daughter. Late one night, the young
girl fled to our house for protection from him.
My brother and I were in bed and my mother
answered the door. The poor girl was terrified*

and begged for help. My mother took her in. Her father broke into our house in pursuit of his daughter. My mother stuck her .38 caliber revolver in his ribs and told him he would never lay a hand on her again. He left as quickly as he came. The next day, my mom bought the girl a bus ticket and gave her enough money to last a month. She went to live with relatives somewhere. We never heard from her again.

I WANTED TO fight to make a difference to my country and to avenge the wrong that had been done. My father's fighting spirit and my mother's desire to protect were bred into me. I had no control over that much. What to do with the combination of traits was up to me. They may have been a blessing or a curse. Whichever they were, they wanted a piece of the Japanese.

Camp Catlin was simply another necessary step to advance me in the direction of the war. It was at Camp Catlin I nearly met my downfall. When my outfit moved out to invade Tarawa, I was left behind. I would later find out why. In correspondence to a girl back home in Swan Quarter, North Carolina, I mentioned my age as being fifteen. Letters coming into Hawaii were not censored by the military. However, letters going out were; I had forgotten that. My cover blown, I was immediately summoned to Pearl Harbor.

The colonel at Pearl told me he knew I was fifteen. He explained the Marine Corps was preparing to discharge me. He asked, "Does your mother not object to you being here?" I assured him my mother had agreed not to extradite me from the Marine Corps, as long as I agreed to finish school upon my return. Furthermore, if he did send me home, I would join the Army and give them the benefit of all my excellent Marine training. I was not sent home. However, because of my age, he would not send me into combat either. Accordingly, I was spared Tarawa. Fate had interceded and plucked me from the path to Tarawa and set me on a new course, one that would lead me into an entirely different battle.

The battle for Tarawa, D Day, November 20, 1943, was a pivotal event in the war in the Pacific. Tarawa was the first modern amphibious assault against a well-defended beachhead in the Pacific Theater. It taught the Marines two valuable lessons: First, naval gunfire and aerial bombardments were less effective against man-made fortifications than first thought. Second, Marine and naval planners should never again underestimate the Japanese's will to fight to the last man. The Japanese commander at Tarawa, convinced his defenses were impenetrable, stated, "A million men cannot take Tarawa in a hundred years." The United States Marines conquered the "unconquerable" in just four days.

The fierce struggle for Tarawa was described as "utmost savagery." The Marines suffered heavy casualties, losing more than one thousand men. Out of the 4,800 Japanese defenders, only seventeen remained alive on November 23, when the battle ended.

Missing out on Tarawa left me deeply disappointed. As a further insult, I was given the not-so-glamorous job of driving a trash truck for the Sixth Base Depot. The depot was located halfway between Pearl Harbor and Honolulu. Many supplies were coming into Pearl, and once they were uncrated, it was my duty to haul off the packing material. With the disclosure of my youth, the prospect of getting into battle was farther away than ever, unless I happened upon some crazy Japanese flier with a fetish for attacking trash trucks.

THE ISLANDS WERE a veritable paradise with a lot to offer a young man. One night in Honolulu I saw servicemen lined up in front of a building. I thought they were going to a movie, and judging by the vast numbers waiting to get in, it must have been a popular show. I stood in line to buy my ticket, only to discover the establishment was a government-run brothel employing beautiful, and very capable, stateside ladies; three minutes for three dollars.

While driving along my route one day, I stopped at a roadside service station for a break. As a result of the war, there was no fuel available, but there were drinks and light snacks. Just outside the front door, I leaned against a cooler and took my time unwrapping a chocolate bar. There was no hurry; the dumpsite I was en route to would still be there when I got to it. Looking toward the vacant lot next door, my eye caught sight of a car up on blocks. She was not just any car; she was a black 1935 Auburn convertible. The attendant told me a millionaire had left her behind shortly after the Japanese attack. The size of a Duesenberg, with chrome pipes off the hood, spare tires on the fenders, and a town and country horn, she was a beautiful machine and could be mine for 150 dollars.

I had two close buddies back in camp. They both had the same last name—Ward—though they were not related to each other. The three of us hastily pooled our funds and purchased the automobile. I borrowed four tires from supply, and to prevent any misunderstanding with the military, promptly filed off the serial numbers. A quick trip to the canvas shop produced a brand-new top. She was not only beautiful, but also big enough to seat four Marines abreast in one seat. She had no license, and likewise, neither did I. It made no difference; I was never stopped by law enforcement. At every opportunity, my buddies and I cruised around the island in her, attended some pretty wild luaus, and had a wonderful time. None of the guys back home had anything like her. We drove along the shoreline with the top down, having a ball. I tried to remember when I had enjoyed a ride so much.

One Christmas morning I awoke to find a saddle under the tree. Right after, my father surprised me with a pony and a cart he purchased from my uncle, Frank, the same uncle that gave me the Marine hat. I named the pony Charlie.

For many joyous hours Charlie trotted up and down the sandy dirt roads of Plymouth, North Carolina, carrying my friends and me in the cart he pulled behind. Sometimes other neighborhood kids brought their horses and mules to our farm to play cowboys and Indians. I loved to be the Indian and hold on to Charlie's mane, get him running, and jump on his back, a maneuver I had seen skillfully executed by the cowboy star, Tom Mix. Other children would chase me around on their mounts and then our roles would be reversed.

Charlie and I shared many happy days riding in the woods, across town to my grandfather's farm or to see my buddy, Marshall Moore. Marshall often rode his pony with Charlie and me. He was a good friend who enjoyed life much the same as I.

Marshall grew from the kid that used to race me down the road in front of my house to a fine young man. Unfortunately, he never lived to be an old man. He went to work in the paper mill, the manufacturer that kept Plymouth alive in those days. I have never been quite sure of what occurred on the day Marshall had his accident. Somehow he was pulled in between two industrial rollers and fatally injured, living only long enough to instruct a co-worker to tell his mother he would not be coming home. The whole community was saddened by the loss. It was a front-page story for days.

That was Marshall's eventual fate, but in

my fondest memories, Marshall and I ride our ponies headlong into the ocean breeze to thrill our hearts with the sensation that we were riding faster than we actually were.

I APPRECIATED THE liberty bestowed on me as a child to play and work on my own initiative. It taught me responsibility and independence. The elation of freedom was indescribable, but that was a lifetime ago. Once, life was good. After my father died, nothing ever held the same sweetness for me again.

When my father passed away, I grew bitter. Other boys had a father and it hurt me that I had lost mine. With no father to guide me, I stayed in trouble a lot. I would fight anyone over anything. My mom was constantly receiving bad reports on me from school, mostly concerning fighting. When I knocked a girl down for pestering me, my mother decided she'd had enough and I was too much for her, my mother, to handle. Additionally, I was an obstacle to any prospective suitor that came to call on the young widowed Lucas. She was only thirty-five years old when my father died, and because of her extraordinary beauty, was very much sought after. She packed me off to Edwards Military Institute hoping military school would instill some discipline in me. I was happy enough at Edwards. Due to the loss of my father and my mother's search for a new husband, I felt disconnected from the family I was born into. School, and eventually the Marines, became my family. I always felt I belonged to the Corps, and it belonged to me.

My next assignment was a camp located between Pearl Harbor and Camp Catlin, aptly named Tent City. The military had assigned me to safe duty, which did not fit into my plan. Somehow I had to get into the fight, and it was not going to happen unless some changes took place. By observation, I had discovered Marines getting sent into combat areas if they caused trouble and created problems for the military. I could do that. I had been known to be a problem in the past; it was something at which I was truly gifted. The time had come for me to be enough of a headache that my superiors would send me into action just to get me out of their hair. If everything went according to plan, in no time at all I would be handing out my own brand of discipline to the Japanese, one body count at a time. During my next seventeen liberties I got in seventeen fights and was locked up seventeen times.

On one occasion, in the summer of 1944, I came off liberty and returned to Tent City about half smashed. I needed a light for my cigarette. While walking down one of the tent rows, I encountered a Marine. He was the body-builder pretty-boy type. Anytime command needed an official escort for public relations duty, Pretty-Boy was their man. I do not know why. I was kind of short, but thought I looked as good as he did. I asked him for a light. Pretty-Boy responded sarcastically, "I don't serve the public with matches." I bumped him out of my way, entered his tent, and began tossing its contents all over. The situation got nastier. Furious, he got in my face and called me a "runt." I felt that old familiar twinge, like someone lighting my fuse. It was a short fuse, and when it ignited, so did I. His face got messed up a little in the fight. He immediately jumped up and ran to the head to check his appearance for any damage. That is what concerned him the most—his looks. His pretty face was ruined. He was so angry, he hit the wall with his fist and thereby suffered a more extensive injury than any I had inflicted.

As a result of that incident I was locked up for forty-five days in the brig awaiting court martial. I pounded rocks twelve hours a day. The hammer I used had a .50 caliber handle. As each swing came in contact with a rock, the vibration caused severe jarring to my body. My hands were blistered and sore; every muscle and joint ached. I hated the punishment. By the end of the day, I welcomed the dark comfort of my four-by-eight jail cell. Following my court martial, I received a sentence of thirty days on bread and water. Prisoners were served two slices of bread and a glass of water, three times a day. On every fifth day, inmates were allowed out of their cells to receive a healthier, more conventional meal.

Every brig had an ape of a sergeant, and the one I had a run-in with was as insufferable and mean as they come. He was from Texas, a hulking man on the outside and gutless on the inside. He routinely brutalized the prisoners. One of his preferred tortures was to keep inmates up all night scrubbing asphalt. The sergeant barked, "You're gonna' scrub it 'til it's white!" This torturous activity was followed the next day by twelve more hours of rock hammering.

Cigarettes were considered contraband, and somehow they were making their way into the brig. The sergeant was determined to find out how they were getting in. I was escorted to a room where the contemptible Sergeant Ape instructed a guard to hold a .45 caliber handgun on me. The sergeant said if I offered any resistance, the guard would kill me and would further report that I attempted to escape. In an effort to force me to give up information about the contraband I was tortured repeatedly. The sergeant made me fold my arms in front, "Indian style," while he beat me in the stomach, time and time again. When I doubled over, he made me straighten myself up and the assault was repeated.

I was assigned an empty cell with nothing but a blanket to wrap around me. I slept on the floor. At thirty-minute intervals I was removed from the cell and taken out in the street. He ordered me to scrub the asphalt with a brush for thirty minutes and then I was returned to my cell. Thirty minutes later I was awakened and once again taken to the street. This continued all night long for several nights in a row.

I never told him anything. Actually, that is not entirely true. The day after I was released, I returned to the brig and told him he was a "big, yellow, bastard Texan" and that I was there to beat his ass. It takes a coward to beat up on a defenseless person. He refused to face me and never had the courage to meet my challenge. Five days later, I wound up back in the same brig.

I am not sure how many bottles of beer were kept in the ship's stores, but from all appearances, there must have been a million. In May of 1944, to celebrate my recent release from the brig, my buddies, the same ones that helped purchase the Auburn, and I shanghaied a truck from the motor pool. We drove to the Honolulu docks and commandeered enough brew to fill ten thirty-gallon GI cans. Ice from the chow hall completed the haul. It was enough to supply the whole company. After everyone was good and drunk, we were encouraged to return for another load. Our judgments were somewhat dulled and it sounded like a good idea at the time. The Marine driving the truck into the warehouse was so inebriated, he rammed us into a large pallet of beer which resulted in a tremendous crash. Bottles were exploding, spewing, and popping in every direction. We all three uttered the same expletive in unison.

Hawaiians working security came running from everywhere and the shrill of MP whistles bounced off the walls of the storage facility. The Shore Patrol pursued my two buddies, who had bolted from either side of the vehicle. I had been sitting in the middle seat and could not make good my escape. I was detained until a vehicle arrived to transport me to the brig. An army MP was questioning me and filling out some forms. I handled the situation with all the skill of a well-trained Marine. When asked for my name, I supplied a false one, and in response to each question, I lied. In the distance, I saw my partners in crime hiding around the side of a warehouse and thought I heard them yell the words, "Hit him!" I am not sure if that is what they said, but that is exactly what I did. I hit him, grabbed his carbine, and ran like hell.

I exited the warehouse and covered a fair amount of ground before rounding a corner and ducking into another warehouse. At least, that is what I thought I was doing. If going back for more beer was my first mistake, running into that particular building was my second. It was the same warehouse I had just run out of! And by this time, it was full of angry military police and shore patrolmen.

I was not fortunate enough to escape again. I dropped the carbine to surrender to the authorities and was directed to a nearby office. A Hawaiian cop kicked me in the rear. I told him if he did that again, I would kill him. He barked, "I'll shoot you!" I replied, "You'll have to!" I was immediately incarcerated in the same brig from which I had just been discharged five days before.

Sergeant Ape and I eyeballed each other, but I had no more trouble from him. Every day the MPs loaded me up and took me to Tent City in an effort to identify the other Marines involved in the heist. I was not about to inform on anyone, but the daily routine of reviewing troops was more fun than being locked up or pounding rocks, so I played along. Eventually, the MPs tired of the situation and gave up. For forty-five days I worked the rock pile awaiting another court martial. Following my conviction, I was sentenced to thirty more days on bread and water, served three times a day.

Across the street from the brig was another prison. Inside the facility's barbed wire were Japanese prisoners of war. The enemy spent their imprisonment lying on cots, reading magazines, and eating three square meals a day. It made no sense to me, and thoughts of their luxury compared to my lack of it increased my contempt for the Japanese even more. I had spent a total of five months in the brig. I had already waited too long for my shot at them; the wait was over.

Tokyo Rose was broadcasting information about troop ships assembling in Hawaii in preparation of an invasion. The 5th Division was anchored at Pearl Harbor and the 4th Division was seventy-five miles southeast at Maui. My cousin was in the 5th Division, 1st Battalion, and 26th Regiment. I told my buddies I was going to join a combat outfit. Taking only a single set of fatigues and a pair of boots rolled up and carried under my arm, I walked away from Tent City, leaving behind all my personal belongings, as well as my prized 1935 Auburn convertible. I never looked back.

6

Stowaway

In the truest sense, freedom cannot be bestowed; it must be achieved.
— President Franklin D. Roosevelt

Pearl Harbor bristled with military activity. Ships were constantly coming and going. I went there often in my spare time. On more than one occasion, I had taken a moment and thoughtfully scanned the famed harbor in an attempt to visualize the assault and the horrors experienced by our troops on that fateful December morning.

The Japanese attack on Pearl Harbor, Hawaii, on December 7, 1941, stunned millions. United States intelligence had known for some time that Japan was planning an assault, but no one knew when or where. Enemy planes, launched from their carriers, began the bombing raid at 0755 hours, Pacific time. One hundred eighty-three Japanese planes struck American airfields on the island of Oahu before turning their attention to the harbor. Battleships, moored along "Battleship Row," were the primary targets of the first wave. Ten minutes into the battle a bomb crashed through the *Arizona's* two armored decks igniting its magazine. Within minutes she sank to the harbor floor, taking 1,177 lives with her. A second wave of 170 planes completed the mission. When the attack ended two hours later, 188 of the United States's aircraft had been completely destroyed and 159 more were damaged. Five battleships were on the ocean floor, sixteen warships had suffered major damage, 2,400 American military were dead, and another 1,100 men were wounded.

The casualties at Pearl Harbor suffered from many different types of injuries. Men suffered gunshot wounds to the head, neck, body, and extremities. There were varying degrees of injuries caused by shell and shrapnel; penetrating abdominal wounds; traumatic amputations; wounds containing foreign matter; and bone fractures. Severe burns were caused by flaming fuel oil. Some of the injured suffered from "flash burns," the result of intense heat from exploding bombs. Many were treated for asphyxia. Almost all victims suffered from varying degrees of shock. The horrors that occurred on December 7, 1941, inspired the battle cry that spurred each and every American to pull together as one and to defeat the Empire of Japan: "Remember Pearl Harbor!"

Damaged vessels that could be restored were either back in service or being refitted. Ships beyond repair stood vigil in the harbor, an ever-present reminder of the enormity of the attack. Halawa Cemetery was not far away. There on the heights, in neat orderly rows, small white grave markers stood like little sentries, keeping watch in silent reverence as our heroes slept. Burial of the Pearl Harbor dead began on December 8, 1941. Some of the dead were buried here in Halawa Cemetery, and others laid to rest in Honolulu at Oahu Cemetery. The Chaplain Corps provided two officers who, along with two civilian priests, rendered proper religious rites at the hospital and again at the gravesites. Funeral ceremonies were held each afternoon in the Oahu and Halawa Cemeteries. The brief military ceremony included a salute fired by a Marine guard and the playing of taps by a Marine bugler. As I stood quietly by the neat mounds that marked each grave I made a solemn vow to those men and reaffirmed that pledge time and time again; I would do everything humanly possible to avenge their murders.

Hundreds of servicemen were coming into Honolulu on liberty from the armada of more than two hundred ships, moored four abreast in the harbor. Such a display of sheer naval power was breathtaking. Ships were often in the harbor, but not in such extraordinary numbers. It was obvious something big was up. An opportune moment like this had never before presented itself to me and I feared it might not again. Somewhere out there was my cousin, Oliver Lucas, and the ship he was assigned to was preparing for action. That is where I wanted to be, but I had absolutely no idea how to locate him.

Men on liberty were being shuttled to and from their ships in Higgins boats. As one boatload prepared to leave the dock, I sauntered onboard like I knew where I was going. A Marine told me there were 5th Division Marines on the ship to which he was en route. When the Higgins boat stopped at the first ship, I followed him up the gangway, saluted, and stepped aboard APA160, the USS *Deuel*.

Inquiries about Oliver Lucas hit pay dirt almost immediately. A Marine said, "You mean Sam Lucas? This is his ship!" Back home, we never referred to Oliver as "Sam"; that was his middle name. It did not matter; he was the one and the same. I was informed that Sam was on liberty, but he had to be back before dark. What are the chances, of all the ships I could have landed on, I picked the right one the first try? I passed the time by strolling the deck and keeping an eye out for Sam. At the time I was unaware that he was already onboard and getting some stitches in his scalp, eight of them. Seems that Sam had run into a little problem on shore leave. I had lost count of how many times accidents like that had happened to me while on liberty.

A shipmate saw my cousin below deck and told him I was on board. Sam left sickbay as soon as he could get away and quickly located me on the weather deck. Sam looked like the rest of the Lucas family. Though taller, Sam was not as big a man as I, but he was stout and full of the Lucas fighting spirit. I smiled when I saw him and asked if he was surprised to see me. He said, "Nothing you'd do would surprise me, Jack!" Sam told me he had sailed on the *Deuel* from San Diego to Pearl. We talked until daylight faded into dark. He advised me it was time to go ashore. I said, "I'm not going ashore. I'm going wherever this ship is going." Sam's brown eyes gleamed at the prospect of what was ahead for us. We both knew something big was getting ready to happen and this convoy was poised to be a part of it.

I had always assigned myself where I wanted to go in the Marine Corps and this latest appointment topped them all. I was well pleased with my new reassignment. The steps I had taken were awkward, but necessary. It may have been the ignorance of youth, inexperience, or raw courage that drove me. Whatever the reason, I was absolutely certain my actions were the correct ones, and with each breath and beat of my heart, I was sailing closer and closer to an enemy I had sworn to kill. I was delighted to be attached to the newly formed 5th Division.

The 5th Marine Division was activated on January 21, 1944. More than nine thousand Marines of the 5th Division were killed or wounded in the thirty-six day assault on Iwo Jima. Fourteen Medals of Honor and ninety-three Navy Crosses were awarded among 5th Division Marines.

THE NEXT DAY, January 10, 1945, the USS *Deuel* weighed anchor and steamed out of the harbor, destined for battle. Ahead of me lay the prospect of new adventures. However, trailing farther and farther behind, virtually unnoticed, were the final scattered remnants of my child-hood rapidly floating away in my wake. I had embarked on a perilous journey that would reveal to me images of the sort never intended for such youthful eyes and it would occur all too soon.

With hundreds of men on board I was easily absorbed into the environment. I kept mostly to myself, taking few individuals into my confidence. As a rule, daily tasks were performed in units. Marines slept, showered, and ate with their units. Being a stowaway, I had no unit. Therefore, a little creativity was necessary on my part. Watching the routine of the ship, I learned if you were on guard duty you went to the front of the chow line and ate first. More importantly, you were not expected to sit with any particular unit. This worked very well for me. At some point, a comment was made about my having a tough sergeant who put me on guard duty so often. I responded that the sergeant did not like me very much and he put me on guard duty to keep me out of his sight. Sam and his buddies slipped food to me when they could.

Everyone took saltwater baths unless the ship turned on the soft water for bathing and that was rare. To laun-der my clothing, I tied my fatigues to the end of a rope and rinsed them in the sea. Afterward, I hung them up to dry in front of the big blowers on top deck. Wearing clothes washed in saltwater was not so bad, but washing myself in saltwater was miserable.

Men sunned themselves on the deck during the day, played cards, shot craps, exercised, and wrote letters home. I did not write home often. My home was with the Marines. To ease the anxiety of the impending battle, weapons and ammunition were checked and rechecked and many war stories shared.

Some men chose to sleep topside, especially on warmer nights when the heat made sleeping below in the still stagnant air too uncomfortable. Without a bunk assignment, I had no choice but to sleep on deck. Higgins boats were stacked three high. Sam told me the sentries always checked the bottom two, but never the third one on top. Each evening Sam and I made the climb to the uppermost boat, crawled in, and got comfortable for the night. No one was ever the wiser. Topside was unpleasant on cooler nights. As a result, I would sit in the head for an hour or so, to get warm. If I had stayed any longer, other Marines would have gotten suspicious, and stowaway or not, I had a reputation to maintain.

Even if I had had a bunk, I would have preferred sleeping in the open. Nighttime on the ocean was spectacular. Each night I gazed in amazement of earth's moon, surrounded by the blackest of night sky, dotted with millions of brilliantly lit stars. Nighttime on the sea was beautiful. Sam and I enjoyed sleeping under the stars, just as our fathers had before us.

When my father was a small boy, a storm toppled the chimney of the family home. It crashed through the ceiling of his bedroom, opening a view to the sky above. Since new construction of the house was already planned for the following spring, the roof and ceiling were not repaired. My father's parents began moving the furniture out of the damaged room and intended to simply shut that living space off until it was time to rebuild. Our fathers begged to be allowed to stay in the room so they could sleep under the stars.

Reluctantly, their parents conceded and my father and his brother, Sam Lucas, remained in the room. They watched the seasons change from atop homemade goose down beds. In fall, the leaves gathered in the corner of their room. As winter settled in along the Atlantic coast, they kept themselves tightly wrapped in their mother's hand-stitched quilts, and watched delightedly at the pyramid of snow forming un-

der the open skylight in their room. My father loved the open sky and appreciated the damage to his room that allowed him the sensation of sleeping outdoors. I can only imagine when the elements that entered his living space changed from ice to warm spring rain he was saddened the adventure was coming to an end.

I UNDERSTOOD HOW Dad felt. That was part of his legacy to me, an appreciation for simple things. Like him, I enjoyed warm sunny days, lazy afternoons fishing off the docks, and sleeping under God's glorious heavens. I felt the cool sea-spray blow across my face. I wondered if, like my father's, my adventure was coming to an end or whether it was just beginning.

Sam's friends had warned me that after thirty days AWOL, I would be reclassified a deserter. My picture would go up in post offices nationwide and my poor mama would faint at the sight of my name and face on a wanted poster. If I turned myself in, would they brig me or would I be allowed to go into battle? If I went into battle, what would the outcome be for me, and what would the outcome be for my buddies, the battle, and the country?

From where I lay, looking out into space, the universe appeared so peaceful. If anyone up there was looking back, they would not see a similar peace. After more than three years of fighting, the whole world was still at war. The Allies would be fighting Germany for three more months, and Japan for almost six. Thoughts clogged my mind; it was mentally exhausting. I fell asleep attempting to sort out all the possibilities.

It was 1530 hours on February 8, 1945, when I decided it was time to set things straight. I turned myself in to Captain Robert Dunlap. It was our twenty-ninth day at sea. He escorted me to Lieutenant Colonel Dan Pollock's quarters. Standing as erect as possible in front of the lieutenant colonel, I awaited his judgment. He said, "Young fella', you're causing me a lot of administrative trouble, but I sure wish I had a whole boatload of men that wanted to fight as bad as you do." Captain Dunlap asked the lieutenant colonel, "Where do I assign him?" I volunteered that I would like to be assigned to my cousin's outfit, the 1/26th. Lieutenant Colonel Pollock said, "Put him in there!"

I had indeed created an administrative nightmare. In addition to the problems I was causing on board the *Deuel*, I had left my former post in Tent City where men were now dealing with the snafu on that end too. This was a wonderful and proud moment for me. Thanks to Colonel Pollock, I was finally within reach of my goal. He had no way of knowing the Marine he had just positioned for action was only sixteen years old.

Officially, I was classified deserter and reduced in rank to private on February 10, 1945, exactly thirty days after I went AWOL. The deserter classification remained until Colonel Pollock's report caught up with my records. The mark was removed February 26, 1945, and my rank of private first class restored.

After Captain Dunlap and I left Lieutenant Colonel Pollock's quarters, the captain took me to the bow of the ship for a photo and a Marine photographer casually snapped our picture. It was not an uncommon occurrence. In addition to battle photos, Marine photographers often recorded servicemen in performance of their daily routine, but there was something very unusual about this seemingly innocuous incident. Standing together on the deck, bathed in that instantaneous flash, we shared a fraction of an exceptional moment. In that mere wisp of time, I experienced a phenomenon that was electrifying and chilling, as well as comforting and enlightening. Never before had I felt such an overwhelming sense of well-being. It embraced me fully, totally, and completely. The sensation defied explanation and understanding. It just was. In this fragment of an instant, it became abundantly clear to me that I would not be killed in battle, and something spectacular would happen not only to me, but to Captain Dunlap as well.

On February 20 and 21, 1945, on the island of Iwo Jima, Captain Robert Dunlap, a twenty-four-year-old Illinois farmer, crawled more than two hundred yards forward of the lines to spot enemy emplacements. He remained forward for two nights, calling in artillery fire. Five days later, he was cut down by a rifle round to the hip. Captain Dunlap survived, but his fighting days were over. More than any other single action, Captain Dunlap's daring, an undertaking for which he would receive the Medal of Honor, accomplished the clearing of Iwo's western beaches.

WE ANCHORED OFF Saipan, in Magicienne Bay. The *Deuel* was one of more than five hundred ships waiting to sail the final six hundred miles to Iwo Jima. A Marine was taken ashore with appendicitis and I was issued his rifle and gear. Before the armada left Saipan we performed a practice landing. Troops scrambled down the landing nets and boarded Higgins boats that had been offloaded into the bay. The landing crafts circled and made a run toward shore. Air support flew low over mock fortifications on the beach. Just before reaching land, our Higgins boats veered away and returned to the ships.

Two days later, at dawn's first light, the *Deuel* weighed anchor and headed north. Once we were far enough out to sea, we were informed our destination was Iwo Jima, and the expectation was that the island could be taken in three days. That was the expectation, but not the reality.

I had never heard of Iwo Jima; neither had anyone else. I did not care where it was as long as there were Japanese to shoot at when we got there. For months the island had been bombed daily by B-29s and the navy's big guns had pounded it relentlessly for two weeks. We had no way of knowing what little effect that bombardment had had on the island.

Located halfway between Saipan and Tokyo, Iwo Jima had the only adequate landing site in the region for large planes. The United States desperately needed a foothold on the island for their B-29 bombers and smaller shorter-range fighter escorts. Up until this point in the war, B-29s were forced to fly from the Marianas to Japan, and return without benefit of fighter escorts. As a result, bombers in trouble with no place to land were lost. If the United States could establish an airfield close enough to Japan, the B-29s could carry less fuel and more bombs.

Japanese fighter planes stationed on Iwo were capable of intercepting unescorted B-29s on bombing missions. To further inhibit American efforts, Iwo had a radar station capable of giving up to two hours' warning of an impending B-29 raid on the Japanese mainland. Strategically, Iwo Jima was important to both sides. In order to protect its mainland, it was imperative Japan maintain control of the island, and this resolve was demonstrated by the more than twenty thousand enemy soldiers embedded there.

In late May 1944, General Hideki Tojo summoned General Tadamichi Kuribayashi to his office in Tokyo and assigned him the task of defending the island of Iwo Jima. Kuribayashi was not sent to save the island, only to hold it for as long as possible and that meant until death. It would have taken ships and guns for the Japanese to hold on to Iwo, and Kuribayashi had only guns and men.

The defense of the island was the culmination of careful and precise planning. Specialists came from Japan and took measurements, tested the soil, and drew blueprints for fortifications. There were numerous natural caves honey-combing the island and modifications were made with hand tools in the soft volcanic limestone creating a network of tunnels all over the island. The specialists knew how to form them to neutralize shock blasts near the openings. The official design called for caves to be constructed five feet wide, five feet high, at least thirty-five feet long, and no less than thirty feet below the surface. Openings were angled at ninety degrees a few feet inside for protection from flamethrowers, artillery, and satchel charges.

By the time the Marines landed, the island was connected from one end to the other by myriad caves and tunnels. Located underground was Kuribayashi's command headquarters, communications, and coding, and piped-in electricity, steam, and water. All sensitive areas were reinforced with concrete. The Japanese had enough food supplies to last seventy-five days, and with rationing, even longer. The island was well fortified with more than six hundred concrete pillboxes designed to enable their weapons to be fired in any direction. Big guns were implanted in re-formed natural caves. Every square foot of the island was in range of enemy weapons.

Previous allied landings had demonstrated to General Kuribayashi that no beach defense could hold against the

Americans. Therefore, artillery was ordered to the north or hidden at the base of Mount Suribachi. One hundred sixty-five concrete pillboxes and two hundred caves defended the mountain. Kuribayashi would hold his main forces in these locations and exact the highest toll of Marine casualties as possible. If he had to give up the island, it was to be at the greatest cost to the Americans.

In November of 1944, the United States forces began softening up the island. By D Day, February 19, 1945, 6,800 tons of bombs and twenty-two thousand naval shells had been dropped on Iwo Jima by the Americans. This process would later prove to be ineffective, eliminating comparatively few enemy soldiers. With over twenty thousand Japanese defenders and an additional American landing force of seventy-four thousand, Iwo Jima would be the most populated eight square miles on earth. The battle to control it would be fought in a primitive style, with satchel charges, rifles, bayonets, and flamethrowers. After months of preparation, the enemy was ready and lying in wait for the invasion of Marines.

On the morning of D Day, I went on guard duty at 2400 hours. I was assigned a post in the hold of the ship, guarding supplies. Reveille sounded at 0300 hours. Few men had slept. At 0400 hours I was coming off duty. Standing watch in the smothering cargo hold drenched my clothing with sweat. My clothing adhered to every inch of my body. An hour late for breakfast, I missed out on the steak and brandy that was served with eggs that morning. By the time I got to eat, eggs were all that remained. Steak was not served every day, only that one morning, like an ominous last meal.

I looked up and down the rows of young men wolfing down their chow. For some, this would be their last morning. For the remainder, every morning hereafter would be forever changed. During the night, while most men had slept in their bunks, the *Deuel* had steamed her way toward the little postage stamp–size island that now loomed off our bow. Like a lighted city, Iwo Jima shone bright in the darkness. Mushrooming high above sea level, Mount Suribachi was most visible and it glowed from the relentless shelling. The enemy could not be seen, but they were there, more than twenty thousand of them, dug in deep in the bowels of the island, well fortified against our assault. My chance to see them up close would come, and soon.

I had a score to settle with Japan and all I wanted was an opportunity to do my little part. I wanted it for the families of the slaughtered and wounded at Pearl Harbor. I was on fire inside and ready to explode at the first opportunity to draw blood. I was not afraid; I came here to kill, not to be killed. As I stood on the deck of the *Deuel*, looking toward the distant glittering mushroom that was Iwo Jima, I was five days into my seventeenth year.

The order came at 0630 hours. "Land the landing force!" We assembled on the weather deck and prepared to load the Higgins boats that sailors were lowering on their davits. The first wave troops loaded into amphibious tractors, called Amtracs, stowed in the bellies of landing ship tanks (LSTs). When the time came, the Amtracs would be launched from the LSTs and navigate in huge circles with other Amtracs, a necessary maneuver to perform in order to maintain our position against the ocean's currents. When further ordered, we would break from the circle and make our way to the landing site.

Naval fire began at 0640 hours. Heavy shelling continued for nearly an hour and a half, dropping thousands of tons of explosives on the island. Each explosion resulted in a brilliant orange flash, followed by billowing black ash that hung over the island like a dark cloud. Rocket-launching gunboats slammed 9,500 of their roaring missiles into the cliffs around an area of the island known as "the quarry." It was an awesome sight to behold. At 0805 hours, all firing ceased.

Aerial bombardment began. Seventy-two navy fighters and bombers made low-level, three hundred mile per hour strafing and bombing runs. They made numerous passes on the beaches, terraces, and hills. When the navy pilots returned to the carriers to rearm and refuel, the Marine pilots, waiting their turn from five thousand feet above, took over the process of softening up the island in their Corsairs. When the aerial assault was complete, the navy's big guns opened up on Iwo once more. In the thirty-five minutes from 0825 hours until H-Hour, eight thousand shells battered the landing zones.

The day before—February 18, 1945—we had been issued ammunition and grenades. As I stood on the weather deck in a light drizzling rain, I checked to make sure my gear was as it should be, grenades, with pins slightly bent, packed with rifle, ammunition, canteen, and my wallet. I tore off a piece of a cardboard ammunition box. On it, I wrote a note which read, *Please send to Mrs. Radford Jones, Belhaven, N.C. That is my mother.* I put the note with my wallet, which held sixteen dollars and pictures from home, and stuffed both into my backpack. I do not remember saying a prayer, nor do I remember anyone else doing so. The Lord would give me an opportunity to do that later.

Those of us new to battle were eagerly talking to Marines who were experienced in combat. The framework of the division was made up of veterans. I talked to them about going into battle. The more I talked to them the more excited I became. They told me to expect fear, but after I got into it, fear would dissipate and I would concentrate on the job at hand.

The fatigues I had been issued were better suited for a "seven-footer" than someone of my five-feet eight-inch stature. The only way to make them fit was to roll the pants' legs up several inches. It did not look quite right, but looks were not important. While everything was not exactly as it should be on the outside, everything was very well squared away on the inside. I was ready; I was born ready.

7

Red Beach Landing

Nothing can stop the man with the right mental attitude from achieving his goal; nothing on earth can help the man with the wrong mental attitude.

—President Thomas Jefferson

In order to board a Higgins boat, Marines had to climb down the side of the ship on a landing net. As each Higgins boat was loaded with Marines, it proceeded to a rendezvous point with other Higgins boats and began navigating in a continuously revolving circle while awaiting the order to land. Sam and I, being of the same unit, were both assigned to the same Higgins boat, which we boarded at 1100 hours. I saw Sam, but we did not speak. It was difficult to communicate over the roar of the engines. In order to be heard, one had to yell, so there was little conversation. Focused on the task ahead, I had nothing to say. The seas were rough and some guys started getting sick. I was not sick or scared. Thirty-eight months had passed since the Japanese attacked Pearl Harbor. It had been an arduous journey and I was anxious to go ashore and finish what I had set out to do. As my vessel took its place among the others in the tactical circle of Higgins boats, I looked back at the *Deuel*. I would not be returning to her. We had separate courses to chart and she had a part of her own to play in history.

On September 2, 1945, the Deuel *would sail into Tokyo Bay, part of a fifteen-mile column intended to impress the Japanese with what they would have been up against had they not surrendered. With all ships dressed in battle flags, it would be an impressive show put on by the allied forces. From the deck of the* Deuel *her crew would be close enough to the USS* Missouri *to see the formal navy whites lined up awaiting the ceremony, and bear witness to the signing of the unconditional surrender*

of Japan. Most impressive would be the sight
of the American flag rippling splendidly in the
breeze high above the deck of the Missouri.
The same banner had flown over the United
States Capitol on Pearl Harbor Day.

THE DEUEL HAD served me well, and I wished the very
best of luck to her and her crew.

With each new island the Allies fought to take back
from the Japanese, the battles increased in ferocity. Iwo
Jima was Japan's front door and the emperor's soldiers
were willing to fight to the death to prevent our having a foothold so close to the island of Japan. A lot of
pre-invasion planning had gone into the landing on Iwo
Jima. Although seas were rougher than anticipated and
the terrain not as expected, the assault on Iwo Jima was
better prepared for than any prior landings.

Some previous beach landings had proven to be disas-
trous for the Americans. On Tarawa, due to ineffective
and obsolete reconnaissance methods, many lives were
lost. Miscalculation of the tides and the danger posed
by unforeseen coral reefs located just below the ocean's
surface prohibited vessels from landing Marines on the
beach. Marines were stranded and forced to disembark

their landing craft as much as five hundred yards from the beach and wade across in the open under intense enemy fire. More Marines were killed when the weight of their gear submerged them after they had stepped into holes created by bombs and mortar shells. Accordingly, the navy learned not to depend on photos and old maps to prepare for their landings. It was imperative to establish Underwater Demolition Teams (UDTs) to perform on-site reconnaissance. This allowed the military to chart approaches to the landing areas and to detonate any obstacles. Just prior to the Marines landing on Iwo Jima, the UDTs thoroughly scouted and mapped the ocean floor to provide invasion planners with the very best possible intelligence.

In preparing for the assault on Iwo Jima, the demolition teams located a few anti-boat mines and destroyed them. No obstacles were found and approaches to the island were discovered to be deep and clear. One missed calculation was the terrain. Geological samples collected in the surf had a different consistency than what was ultimately found on the beaches and dunes. This inaccuracy resulted in unforeseen problems when heavy equipment attempted to negotiate the incline up to the plateau.

At 0857 hours, naval bombardment ceased. The landing forces did not realize that seventy-two consecutive days of aerial attacks and naval bombardment had killed less than two hundred of the enemy, and done very little to prepare the island for the invasion of Marines.

The first assault vehicles touched down on Iwo's shore at 0902 hours. This first wave was made up of steel-sided Amtracs, each equipped with a seventy-five-millimeter howitzer, three crewmen, and three machine guns. Based on pre-landing information, the landing force could not have anticipated the problem the terrain would present to them. As soon as the heavy equipment hit dry land and attempted to scale the forty-five degree incline, the vehicles bogged down in the fine gravel that made up the landscape. Some never made it off the beach. The vehicles that succeeded in negotiating the grade were met with intense mortar fire as they moved inland. The ash would soon prove a hindrance for the troops as well. Amtracs unable to navigate the incline began piling up on the landing beaches, further impairing invasion efforts.

Each wave of Marines was comprised of 1,360 men. The entire landing operation required hundreds of Higgins boats to complete the transports. Marines wore green fatigues and helmets covered with brown camouflage. Some men applied protective cream to their faces as a precaution against a flaming assault. The American striking force was more powerfully supported, better armed, and manned by more experience than any other storm landing in history. The landing force enjoyed a healthy three-to-one preponderance over the occupying force. The initial landing was exclusively 4th and 5th Division Marines. The 3rd Division was held in reserve to be used if needed. By February 24, they were needed.

The plan was to land the first troops on the southeast coast on one of the seven landing zones stretching over two miles of beach, between Mount Suribachi and the East Boat Basin. As soon thereafter as possible, American troops were to move onto the plateau and set up a defensive perimeter. Landing at five-minute intervals, six additional waves of Amtracs loaded with Marines followed. At 0905 hours, the first assault troops landed.

The Marines were amazed at the lack of resistance. They assembled on the beach and received very little enemy fire. The Japanese intended to let the beaches fill up with Americans and then cut them down as they tried to move inland toward the central plateau. At that point, there would be no escape for the Marines.

The ambush was a well-planned defense on Kuribayashi's part. At 1000 hours, with the beaches choked with wreckage and infantry, the Japanese fired signal flares. Suddenly, from underground locations virtually invisible to the Americans, the Japanese opened up with their heavy ordnance. Withering artillery and mortar fire bombarded the beaches. Landing craft, as well as Marines, came under heavy assault. Kuribayashi's fifteen-inch guns opened up, raining death down on the invasion force. More than six thousand men were pinned down on the beaches. Landing craft continued their attempts to land as more and more vehicles sank in the surf and piled up on the beach. Shore parties labored feverishly to keep the beachhead open.

An amphibious assault is an extremely complex operation. The first few minutes can determine the overall success or failure of the mission. On Iwo's shore the scene was one of chaos; heaped and useless vehicles blocked incoming landing craft. In the traditional display of discipline and supreme fighting ability the Corps is known for, the Marines began organizing themselves on the beach. Dividing up into their respective units, they overcame adversity and systematically became one well-organized fighting machine.

The beach was ordered closed around 1300 hours and bulldozers went to work clearing the wreckage. Detonation charges were used as well as winches and brute strength to clear the "logjam" of equipment and reopen the beachhead. For two hours, I waited. Shortly before

1500 hours my division was given the go-ahead. Excitement pounded in my ears and my heart beat as loud as the thunder around me. Clouds of expended gunpowder hung thickly over the island and stung my nostrils as my Higgins boat neared the beach.

By design, Higgins boats are supposed to land Marines on the beach by dropping a ramp that serves double duty as the bow of the vessel. My coxswain was in a hurry to offload us and depart. The boat was in fairly deep water for a landing, and when I stepped off the ramp, I sank into the sea up to my chin. My mind urged me to hurry, but I plodded along, my will to hasten hampered by the weight of my soaked and ill-fitting clothing. I struggled out of the surf and onto the beach. My load was considerable, consisting of a backpack, grenades, ammunition, a ten-pound rifle, and a forty-pound shaped-charge used as an antitank device. I never knew how to operate a shaped-charge, only that I was to carry it for someone who did.

At 1500 hours I hit the beach. When I tried to run my fatigues flopped over my feet, making me look like Charlie Chaplin. It would have been humorous under different circumstances. I hastily withdrew my Bowie knife from its sheath at my side and cut off both legs of the saltwater-soaked pants. One cut was about four inches below the knee and the other somewhere around my calf. It was not a pretty alteration, but appearances were the least of my concern. We were still taking heavy incoming fire as I lay on the beach calculating my next move. I could see small arms rounds hitting the ground in front of me and I imagined a Japanese soldier specifically aiming for me.

I was four years old the first time a gun was leveled in my direction. My parents and I went to Virginia to visit friends. I had lain down on a bed to take a midafternoon nap. A boy, much older than I, was on one side of my bed, and a girl slightly younger than the boy was on the other side. I watched the boy open a drawer in the nightstand and withdraw a .44 caliber handgun. He leveled the weapon and fired a round that passed just over my head, hitting the girl in the arm. She ran out of the house into the yard screaming as blood spewed from the wound. It was a frightening experience. I managed to escape death that night. I hoped I would continue to be as fortunate.

As I HUNKERED down on the beach awaiting orders to move inland, I assessed my surroundings. The island of Iwo Jima was formed by volcanic activity more than 2,600 million years ago. The northern end of the island is made up of a broad, domed volcano called Motoyama. This area is flat and well suited for an airfield. On the southern end of the island stands the half-collapsed volcanic cone, Suribati-yama, or what is better known as Mount Suribachi. Much younger than Motoyama, Suribachi looks more like what a volcano is expected to look like. Suribachi's elevation created an excellent vantage point for the enemy to defend the island. The words Iwo Jima mean "sulphur island," and the presence of the pungent chemical made the atmosphere unpleasant to breathe. Iwo, formed out of ash, rock, and obsidian was ugly in appearance. With little vegetation and a grainy black beach, the island did not appear to be of this world. Were it not for the strategic importance of the island, nobody could ever have wanted to inhabit it.

The loose earth was difficult to negotiate. With each step, my feet sank to my knees in the coarse powder. Like trying to walk on beans, we attempted to move up to the plateau, all the while taking incoming mortar and machine gun fire. Torrents of shells rained down on the beaches and well-positioned defenses discharged deadly fire anywhere the enemy chose. The landing beach was being raked with heavy artillery and antiaircraft weapons. As some Marines scrambled up the terraces they came in deadly contact with land mines. Enemy gunners guaranteed no Marines would advance inland with impunity. Bodies were blown apart, their appendages strewn in every direction. At some point, body parts would be collected and carefully identified for eventual burial.

Lifeless bodies of Marines rolled and tumbled in the surf, washing up on the beach like so many pieces of driftwood. Now colored by the blood of so many dead and dying, Red Beach was true to its name. All around me bodies lay in whatever strange contortions the ebb and flow positioned them. Dodging enemy fire, I dropped to the ground alongside another Marine. His eyes were closed, as if he were sleeping. I could not distinguish the injury that took his young life; only that he was gone.

Thousands of miles away, a family waited anxiously for the next letter from him, a confirmation that he was alive and well. Somewhere, a restless mother peered through her front window watching for the mailman. The same mother had carried this Marine under her heart for nine months. She brought him into the world with all the hopes and aspirations that normally accompany the birth of children. His arrival would have been a blessed event, with relatives and friends coming by his home to meet him and speculate about his life, but never his death. He had a history—a first haircut, trips to the dentist, school, team sports, and a first romance. His loved ones had watched him grow in mind and body until the day he became a man and went to fight for his country. Like all servicemen, he would have received his farewell hugs and handshakes at the train station. He had been duty-bound to ensure that others would have the opportunity to grow up in a free nation as he had. From his seat on board the train, he would have watched as his family, waving from the platform, whispered their prayers and wished him well. Watching him ride away would be their final glimpse of him in life.

A telegram, military official, or clergy would deliver the news. His passing would be his hometown newspaper's front-page story. His parents' anxiety and anticipation would come to an end, as well as all the hopes and dreams of a future with this loved one. There would be no more family gatherings with one hundred-percent attendance. As a constant reminder, a chair would sit empty at the dinner table. One special birthday would forever be remembered, but not celebrated. There would be no more continuation of the family name from his branch of the tree. This young man, the culmination of

Louis Harold Lucas, Jack's father, with Jack and his little Jack Russell terrier, Skippy.

Margaret Edwards Lucas, Jack's mother

Jack Lucas at age ten in Plymouth, North Carolina.

Cadets standing in formation at the Edwards Military Institute, Salemburg, North Carolina, in 1940. Jack Lucas is sixth from left.

Martha and Louis Ed, Jack's younger brother, behind the plow.

Jack (right) and little brother, Louis Ed.

CONSENT OF PARENTS OR GU.   4 TO ENLISTMENT OF A MINOR IN
THE MARINE CORPS

"W. Mrs. Radford Jones _____ and _____ Jones _____

residing in _____ Belhaven _____, County of _____ Beaufort _____

and State of _____ North Carolina _____, do freely consent to the enlistment

JACKLYN HARKEL

of _____ Jack Harold Lucas _____ in the United States Marine Corps as a

(Name in full)
Duration of War

PRIVATE, to serve FOUR YEARS, unless sooner discharged, subject to all the requirements and lawful commands of the officers who may, from time to time, be placed over him; do hereby relinquish all claim to his service, and to any wages or compensation for the same, and do hereby certify that he was born

in _____ PLYMOUTH, N.C. _____ on the _____ 14th _____ day of _____ February _____

19 25 Plymouth

And *I we do solemnly swear (or affirm) that I am the mother and ~~father~~ guardian of the said
I am the legally appointed guardian

Jack Harold Lucas _____, that he has no other legal guardian, and that he has never

(Name in full)

been married, had military service, or been convicted of any crime: So help me God.

(Signature of father or guardian)
Mrs. Radford Jones
(Signature of mother)

ADDRESS (with street and number) _____ East Main St., Belhaven, N.C. _____

Personally appeared before me Mrs. Radford Jones _____ and

_____, residents of Belhaven _____ in the county of

Beaufort _____, and State of North Carolina, each of whom is well known

to me as a credible person, and made oath that the foregoing statement is correct and true, and signed the

same in my presence this 25 day of July, 19 42

G.T. Bilbik Notary Pu.
(Signature of officer administering oath)

my Comm. expire Nov. 12, 1942

*Strike out words which do not apply.

Jack Lucas in the United States Marine Corps at age fourteen.

Jack Lucas's fraudulent enlistment papers showing his year of birth as 1925 instead of his actual birth year 1928.

Jack Lucas at age fourteen.

Jack Lucas (sixth from left) graduated from basic training at Parris Island, South Carolina, in September 1942. *US Marine Corps*

Aerial view of Pearl Harbor, Hawaii. *National Archives*

Jack had this photo made in a souvenir photo booth in Hawaii at age fifteen.

Aerial view of Camp Catlin and Sixth Base Depot on Oahu, Hawaii. *National Archives*

The USS *Deuel* was the vessel on which Jack Lucas stowed away to get to Iwo Jima. *National Archives*

In this view of Iwo Jima you can locate the landing beaches on east side, airfields in the center and Mount Suribachi at the southern tip. A low cloud stretches across Airfield #1 where Jack encountered the grenades. *National Archives*

For the invasion, Marines boarded landing craft by descending nets cast over the sides of ships. *National Archives*

Upon landing, Marines encountered a steep incline. Their progress was hindered by volcanic ash. *National Archives*

Mount Suribachi loomed high above the beaches as Marines made their way up the slopes. *National Archives*

The enemy defended their positions from well-placed fortifications like this one. *National Archives*

Deep trenches leading to enemy quarters were dug into the ground. This trench was not as deep as the one where Jack Lucas encountered the grenades near Airfield One. *National Archives*

Water-cooled machine gun like the one Jack was ordered to retrieve from the beach. *National Archives*

The wounded were evacuated from the beach by Amtrac vehicles.
National Archives

From Amtracs, the wounded were hoisted aboard hospital ships
in wire baskets attached to pulleys. *National Archives*

With Mount Suribachi rising beyond, critically wounded Jack Lucas was
taken aboard the hospital ship, *Samaritan*. *National Archives*

With his right arm still bandaged and his wounds healing, Jack Lucas used his left hand to write a note (upper right in the photo) to his mother at the US Naval Hospital in Charleston, South Carolina. *US Navy*

As he stood on the White House South Lawn, Jack Lucas received this nation's highest combat medal, the Medal of Honor, from President Harry S. Truman. *National Archives*

Jack Lucas smiled through the discomfort as President Truman dug his thumb into his wound. Truman quipped, "I would rather have this medal than be president of the United States." *National Archives*

After the war, Jack Lucas registered for high school at the University of Illinois. *Associated Press*

Jack Lucas is seen here registering for the draft at age eighteen, though he had already received his nation's highest military honor.

After he completed high school, Jack Lucas enrolled in Duke University.

Jack Lucas married Helen Solley Russel on the television program "Bride and Groom" in March of 1952. *Associated Press*

Jack Lucas entered the US Army and joined the paratroopers. *US Army*

First Lieutenant Jack Lucas, US Army, 1962. *US Army*

On May 2, 1963, in the White House Rose Garden, First Lieutenant Jack Lucas met President John F. Kennedy.

At the fiftieth anniversary of the landing on Iwo Jima, February, 19, 1995, Jack Lucas (third from left) was an honored guest, along with two other Medal of Honor recipients, Joe McCarthy and Doug Jacobson (first and second from left). They were accompanied by General Carl E. Mundy, Jr., Commandant of the Marine Corps, and President Bill Clinton. *US Marine Corps*

Following the ceremonies marking the fiftieth anniversary of Iwo Jima, Jack and his family posed with President— and First Lady Clinton.

Jack Lucas (second from left) had a moment to share with (from left to right) Senator John Warner, Senator Bob Dole, and actor Tom Hanks, at the dedication ceremony for the World War II Memorial in Washington in May of 2004.

Jack Lucas in his signature Marine Corps League jacket boarded "his ship," the USS *Iwo Jima,* on August 6, 2004—exactly sixty-two years after his enlistment in the Marine Corps. The officers and crew of the ship stood ready to salute the arrival of the Medal of Honor. *D. K. Drum*

Jack Lucas (left) with his cousin, Samuel Oliver Lucas, at his home in North Carolina. Sam helped Jack stowaway on the USS *Deuel* bound for Iwo Jima. *D. K. Drum*

Jack Lucas met former president Jimmy Carter, during a dedication ceremony for the Robert J. Dole Institute of Politics on July 22, 2003.

As he stood on Red Beach One where he landed sixty years before, Jack Lucas remembered his fallen brothers and the sacrifices they made on Iwo Jima in 1945. *D. K. Drum*

a family's thoughtful and loving guidance, lay heaped in the black volcanic ash on a God-forsaken island in the Pacific. His battle was over.

The lifeless Marine's arm lightly rode each wave as it came to shore and then dropped back to his side as it receded. Back and forth his arm swayed in the surf. It gave the impression he was beckoning his fellow Marines to go forward, to finish the fight for him. He had done all he could.

Marines taking direct hits from mortar rounds were completely evaporated right before my eyes. It was a horrible scene to witness, but giving it much thought would have placed me at further risk. Allowing myself to dwell on the carnage was a luxury I could ill afford. I would think about it later, if I had a later. We had been pinned down for nearly two hours on the beach. Marines dropped all around me; their screams of agony still audible above the shattering violence of relentless explosions. My sole objective was to kill the enemy and I grew frustrated with all the jumping up and down required to evade enemy fire. The way I had it figured, by the time you hear an explosion, it's missed you. If one has your name on it, you never hear it. I wanted to kill the enemy. I knew I had to go forward to do it and that is exactly what I did. Every able man moved forward.

We fought our way up the steep grade to the plateau. I felt like I was making progress, when suddenly, one of the heavy weapons crewmen was killed. A sergeant ordered me and another Marine back to the beach to bring up a water-cooled machine gun. I did not want to backtrack to the beach, but I knew we needed the heavy weapon and I would never defy an order in combat. I had never met the Marine that was helping me. I guess he was from the heavy weapons platoon. It did not matter; we were all brothers. Without hesitation, I returned to the beach through concentrated shelling.

The heavy weapon was on a cart along with several cases of ammunition and water. To allow it to be pulled by two men, the cart was designed with a T-shaped tongue and two spoke wheels like a bicycle's. With each attempt to pull it up the steep grade, the earth moved under my feet and my legs rode the ash back down the incline. The cart's wheels sank deeper as well. Shells exploded all around us. Like trying to walk in a wheat bin, I slid two steps backward with every forward step. I could not have anticipated the ash I cursed on this day would be the very element that saved me the next. Our task was difficult and exhausting. I do not know how we did it, but somehow we managed to get the gun back to the heavy weapons platoon.

The Japanese introduced a new weapon on Iwo Jima, huge 675-pound "spigot" mortars propelled from crude rocket launchers. These were larger shells than most Marines had ever seen. What they lacked in accuracy, they made up for in psychological effect. No American could ever forget the awesome sight of the enormous fifty-five gallon-size drums of explosives, tumbling end over end, screaming through the air. Their travel created an ear-piercing whistle with an accompanying rumble you could feel in your chest. This bombardment usually occurred in the late afternoon. Most of their launches were aimed well over our positions and landed harmlessly in the sea. My cousin Sam referred to this daily ritual as the "evening matinee."

We spent the balance of the day moving across the isthmus of the island, continually dodging heavy artillery and small arms fire. In Hollywood films, you see waves of men advancing on a battlefield. Iwo was not taken that way. We grabbed every bit of cover available to us and moved in fire-team units of four each. From one foxhole to the next, we ran in a crouching position, inching our way toward our objective. I eventually lost sight of Sam and would not see him again on Iwo Jima. I would learn sixty years later that he was never far away from me at any time.

We did not see many Japanese the first day, but our battalion's casualties were heavy, a result of the cut we made across the narrow of the island. Twilight was upon us and we had to prepare for the long night ahead. The four Marines in our fire team attempted to enlarge a crater for us to sleep in. As each scoop of ash was removed, the sides caved in and more ash filled the hole. We dug in as best we could for our first night on Iwo Jima. At 1845 hours, the sun disappeared in the western horizon. Except for the occasional explosion of enemy phosphorous illuminating the sky, darkness descended on the thirty thousand American combat troops ashore.

Just before dawn, if the Japanese held true to form, there would be a banzai charge. For this reason, Marines were ordered to "stay put" in their foxholes, expect anything, and shoot whatever moved above ground. So, we stayed put to keep from getting shot, not only by the Japanese, but possibly by our own men. Unbeknownst to the Americans, Kuribayashi had abandoned the practice of banzai charges, opting instead for a new plan of "ten lives for one." Each Japanese soldier was ordered to kill ten Americans before he was killed. For a while, the Japanese were beating their quota.

English phrases were spoken from somewhere out in the darkness. Phrases such as, "Hey Joe, you ok?" It was an attempt by the enemy to prompt Marines to give away their positions. If you wanted to survive, you ignored them and kept quiet.

We took turns keeping watch in one-hour shifts. I think some of the other guys were a little short on their shift because I was back keeping watch sooner than I should have been. We were tired and it was difficult to sleep through the heavy shelling. Some of Iwo's underground cavities reached temperatures as high as 130 degrees. Marines lucky enough to get in a foxhole close to the subterranean heat kept warm throughout the night. I was not so fortunate. The day was relatively comfortable, but I shivered through the chilly forty-degree hours of darkness.

The night sky was constantly ablaze with a spectacular light show of sizzling flares, accompanied by thunderous shelling. Between explosions the chatter of Japanese soldiers could be heard drifting across the plateau. It was exhilarating to know I had thus far survived. Some people say you are not human if you are not afraid, but I was not afraid. I was apprehensive at times. Perhaps I was too young to appreciate fear.

Nighttime was busy on the beaches. Under cover of darkness the wounded were evacuated, supplies brought in, and more wreckage cleared. Bulldozers cut roads inland and created dugouts to provide protection for aid stations, ammunition, and fuel. Offshore our navy continued with their bombardment of known enemy emplacements.

Tuesday, February 20—D Day plus one—dawned dimly through Iwo's pall of smoldering earth. The weather was mild. Marines were assigned the task of dividing Iwo Jima in two parts in order to isolate Mount Suribachi. The Japanese aptly named the dormant volcano, Suribachi, their word for "cone-shape." Two hundred yards south of my position, Suribachi loomed eerily through the occasional breaks in the clouds created by minute particles of scorched earth. Some divisions were to fight toward the north to take the airfields, while others were ordered to the south to take Suribachi. At first light, my division started moving from the isthmus toward the north end of the island.

Around 1030 hours, the 3rd Battalion of Donn Robertson's 27th Regiment was being decimated to our right by precise and deadly mortar fire. "They died," said Robert Sherrod, a *Time* magazine correspondent, "with the greatest possible violence." There was absolutely nothing that could be done for them and we were instructed to keep moving forward.

Every mound and group of rocks spewed automatic

weapons fire from within. Thanks to American artillery and Sherman tanks, we continued to push forward. The resistance we met was much more aggressive than D Day. During the first eighteen hours of the battle to take Iwo Jima, 2,312 of America's best had fallen. President Roosevelt was reported to have been jolted by the number of casualties and was said to have gasped in horror.

On the plateau my fire team and I spotted an enemy soldier step out from behind some vegetation. Every one of us opened up on him. I had no problem killing him; he would have killed me. An attempt to gather intelligence and souvenirs from his pockets produced an assortment of Japanese currency, postcards, pictures, and a small notebook, whose entries have never been successfully translated. I asked my buddy to tuck the items in my backpack. Accordingly, they were placed with my wallet for safekeeping. The soldier's body suffered no desecration from us and was simply left where it lay.

It was not unusual to see a Marine cut off the little fingers of enemy soldiers and pack them in salt bags to take home as good luck charms. I never did anything like that. I heard there was even worse done to enemy bodies, though that is something I never personally witnessed.

The 5th Marine Division advanced north on the left flank or westerly side of the island, while the 4th Division advanced on the right. We encountered intense concentration of the enemy close to Airfield Number One. Like yellow jackets, the Japanese swarmed in the open. It was unusual to see the enemy above ground. They normally stayed burrowed deep beneath the surface, like vermin, maneuvering via the labyrinth of tunnels and trenches that connected one concrete pillbox to the next. From these fortifications the enemy could dispense deadly fire against the Americans while they remained relatively well protected. The most effective method of capturing these positions proved to be with the use of flamethrowers and satchel charges. Acting out of frustration, some courageous Marines actually charged the pillboxes with grenades, automatic weapons, and raw courage.

We were a team of four, all privates first class: team leader Riley E. Gilbert of Texas, Malvin B. Hagevik of Wisconsin, Allan C. Crowson of Arkansas, and me. A Marine fire team was tactically organized around the Browning Automatic Rifle (BAR). Crowson was our BARman. Gilbert, Hagevik, and I carried standard issue M-1 rifles.

Capable of firing 550 rounds per minute, with an effective range of six hundred yards, the BAR offered an excellent combination of rapid fire and penetration capabilities. At forty-seven inches in length, the shoulder-type weapon was air-cooled, gas-operated, and magazine-fed. A .30 caliber round fired from its chamber traveled 2,800 feet per second. As a result, it became a popular weapon and a tremendous advantage in combat. The BAR, its bipod mount, and a loaded bandoleer weighed a total of forty pounds and required specialized training to operate.

The M-1 rifle had an effective range of 440 yards. Fully loaded, with an eight-round clip and sling, the M-1 weighed a little over eleven pounds and used a .30–06 rifle cartridge. It was a well-constructed elegant looking weapon, carefully shaped from steel and walnut. The M-1 became the first semiautomatic rifle adopted by the United States Military as a standard small arm. It would not only be the weapon of choice in World War II, but in Korea as well.

AROUND NOON OR shortly thereafter, we moved farther north toward Airfield One. We were met with increasing enemy resistance. Captain Dunlap was to our right, directing fire. Our attempts were proving ineffective and we were ordered to cease-fire while Captain Dunlap redirected our offensive.

Immediately, Hagevik led us into a trench. There were two twenty-foot-long trenches, running parallel to each other, approximately four feet apart. The four of us were in one trench. We had no idea what was in the other. From left to right we were lined up respectively—Hagevik first, followed by myself, and Crowson and Gilbert on the far right. Not far away from our position a tank was preparing to fire on a pillbox in close proximity to my team. Like a blazing tongue, flame-throwing tanks could spew burning napalm into the bunkers from distances up to 150 yards and sustain a continuous burn for as long as sixty seconds. I had witnessed what a flamethrower could do to a human body; it was a horrible way to die. Though I had no sympathy for these barbarians who showed no mercy to my countrymen, death by napalm was gut wrenching to watch.

In anticipation of the imminent tank attack, the enemy hurriedly exited the bunker through an adjoining tunnel, which ultimately opened up into the trench across from us. We could not see the men, but they were there. In an effort to reconnoiter, our group leader, Gilbert, made the decision to jump into the other trench. Quite unexpectedly, he landed on one of the fleeing enemy soldiers. Gilbert hastily retreated back to our position. Immediately, the Japanese stood up in front of us and we opened fire.

Possessing rifles forty-three and one-half inches in length and being so close in proximity to the Japanese created a problem. The length of our weapons nearly exceeded the distance between us. We could not fire from the shoulder. Defending ourselves to the best of our ability, we started killing the enemy. I shot two. I have no recollection of the first kill, but the second is still very clear to me. The projectile hit him over the left eye. I watched the blood explode from his forehead in a gush of red. In the next moment, my rifle jammed. M-1 rifles were not known to have this problem; however, the dust and dirt were thick enough to jam even the most reliable weapons. All four of us were actively engaged with the enemy. No one noticed the two grenades drop into the trench in front of Crowson, the BARman. I would have missed them myself had I not been looking downward as I struggled to un-jam my rifle. That is the moment they first caught my eye. Lying at our feet, weighing one pound, less than four inches in length, and with only four seconds of fuse, were the implements of almost certain death. How long had they been there? How much time was left? I yelled, "Grenade!" to alert my buddies and pushed my BARman out of the way.

I remember making the conscious decision to cover the grenades with my body. I knew if they detonated, all of us would have been injured and unable to defend ourselves. The Japanese could easily have finished us off. I had a choice to make and not much time to make it. I could die alone or all four of us would die. The projected outcome for me was no different either way. Jumping on a grenade is not a unique act; everyone knows the result. It was amazing how much thought raced through my head in such a short amount of time.

I dropped to my knees and with a single stroke of my rifle butt, rammed one grenade into the ash. I dove on top of it. Simultaneously, I grabbed the second in my right hand, pulled it underneath me and pushed it into the ash as far as I could. I have a faint recollection of someone running across my back as he hurried to make good his escape. Across my chest hung six grenades of my own. I did not even have the opportunity to shut my eyes. It was fate that put me in harm's way, but it would be faith that saved me.

8

God, Please Save Me

Greater love hath no man than this, that a man
lay down his life for his friends.

—John 15:13

The blast was deafening. One moment I was prostrate
on the ground, and the next, I was floating upward.
With eyes wide open, I watched as my body rose above
the trench floor. From the corner of my eye, I could see
my team running for cover. After the initial blast, silence filled my universe. The peace and tranquility was
euphoric and calming. There was no noise, no pain, no
battle, and no real time, only total and absolute peace.

I never lost consciousness. The force propelled me

into the air, rotating my body 180 degrees. When the momentum had spent itself, I dropped to the earth, landing on my back. My ears began to ring as though I had received a near-knockout punch. Barely audible above the escalating ringing in my ears was the sound of my team finishing off the enemy. My mind struggled to process the muffled noises but everything sounded as though I were underwater. My right arm was pinned underneath me and my first impression was that it had been blown away. Except for an intense tingling sensation, I had no feeling. I was numb all over. I had suffered over 250 entrance wounds. Shrapnel ranging in size from that of a BB to a .22 caliber had riddled the circumference of my body from my head to my thighs. Slivers of wood from the rifle stock were blown into my chest.

Slowly, but surely, I perceived warm blood running down the arm beneath me. As feeling gradually returned to my body, the initial unpleasantness of pain made its presence known, and soon accelerated to an excruciating level finally enveloping me completely in an unrelenting grip of agony.

I detected the distinct taste of blood as it trickled across my tongue, gradually at first, but increasing in volume, until my mouth overflowed with the metallic tasting liquid. Attempting to draw a breath, I sucked blood in with my wind. I choked and gagged, struggling for air. With all the strength I could muster, I forced myself to spit. The fluid gurgled forth and cleared the way for life-giving oxygen. I remained conscious enough to keep my airways free of blood; otherwise, I would have drowned.

My clothes were in shreds and my backpack blown away. I raised my head as much as possible and saw blood spewing from my chest and thigh. I thought, *Is this how it's going to end? Was I meant to survive such an explosion, only to bleed to death afterward? How long does it take for a body to bleed out?* I could not remember. With my flesh in so many tears, would death come quickly?

One lung was punctured, and the sensation that I was suffocating was unbearable. The bleeding was profuse. I pleaded to my Maker, "God, please save me. Please save me, God!" I did not think about Mama or anybody else. I knew on Whom to call. His response to my plea was swift. The heavy bleeding instantly ceased.

Having left me for dead, my team moved on. My rifle was lying beside me with the stock splintered, like a tree that has been struck by lightning. I remembered the grenade I pulled under me was smooth to the touch, like the Japanese percussion grenade. The other, rammed into the ash with my rifle, reacted like a fragmentation grenade, piercing my body many times over. I made these observations rather quickly and under stressful circumstances, but that is my recollection of the devices.

For what seemed like an eternity, I waited for someone to find me, and hopefully, whoever found me would be an ally. The only movement I could make was to wiggle the fingers of my left hand and that took a great deal of effort. Another company was moving up and a Marine approached me. With so much blood and damage to my body and clothing, I was not sure I looked like an American. The Marine saw my movement, recognized me as one of his own, and signaled for a corpsman. The corpsman knelt down beside me, pulled my right arm out from under my body, and we saw that, though it was badly mangled, it was still attached.

Corpsmen carried more than fifty pounds of medical supplies, including bandages, surgical instruments, sulfa, brandy, and morphine. My corpsman also carried a rifle. He immediately started administering morphine and treating my wounds. My right eye was blown out of its socket and lying on my cheek until the corpsman put it back in place. I would later be told the optic nerve had been narrowly missed. The most extensive injuries were to my right side. As the corpsman rendered aid, a Japanese soldier popped out of the tunnel and prepared to lob a grenade at us. Ever on the alert to his surroundings, the corpsman fired at the enemy. As best I could, I muttered, "Kill him! Kill him!" The corpsman emptied his carbine into him and the soldier crumpled to the ground. He had saved my life, twice. Unfortunately, I would learn later, the corpsman himself did not survive Iwo Jima.

We started receiving heavy incoming mortar rounds and everyone was forced to hold their positions. I needed to be evacuated, but stretcher-bearers were unable to reach me due to the heavy barrage. Dirt was being blown over us. It lasted for several minutes. Once the bombardment lifted, the stretcher-bearers moved up and lifted my perforated body onto a litter. I winced at the pain, but did not make any noise. We proceeded toward the beach. Ahead of me lay an immeasurable amount of suffering and misery. Behind me lay eleven dead enemy soldiers in one trench, and in another, one dead enemy soldier, my backpack, and rifle, with its stock broken. Additionally, resting in one of the many footprints in the gray volcanic ash, was the smooth and intact Japanese grenade I had held in my hand. By the grace of God, I had been spared a second explosion.

The stretcher-bearers were tired, but they ran all the way back to the beach with me. The physical as well as the psychological drain of battle had taken its toll on everyone. As I was being transported to the beach, the stretcher-bearer carrying my upper body fell and dropped his end of the litter. My head hit a rock, delivering a deep gash to the back of my skull. I looked up at the Marine. He was exhausted. I knew he was doing the best he could. One more injury mattered little.

The beach was still littered with the wreckage of various landing craft that had fallen prey to enemy shelling and rough seas. Eventually, it would be cleared of the debris to make room for additional landings. Until then, supplies and troops were being brought in with great difficulty.

The military had provided us with a broad range of provisions. Ship-to-shore vessels delivered materials of every conceivable use. Whatever we needed had to be brought in; there were few resources on Iwo Jima. A single Marine required 1,322 pounds of materials to meet his needs. Items being offloaded included everything from paper, pencils, ammunition, matches, maps, clothing, food, and medical supplies, to drinking water, toilet paper, flashlights, blankets, batteries, cigarettes, holy water, and thousands of neatly bundled, white, wooden crosses.

A special Graves Registration Detail landed on D Day. Its main function was the proper cataloguing and interment of the dead. Sites had been predetermined for each of the three division cemeteries. Bodies would go through a specific burial process. One dog tag would be removed, leaving one for burial. If the remains had an index finger, it was to be inked and printed. If there were no hands, bodies would be identified by clothing, tattoos, birthmarks, scars, or any means possible. Each body was to be wrapped in a poncho or blanket and placed in a trench, six feet in depth. Bodies were to be buried three feet from the centerline of one body to the centerline of the next body. Each row would contain fifty bodies and rows were to be placed three feet apart. Graves were to be filled with ash and topped with heavier clay to prevent the ash from blowing away. A wooden form would aid in mounding the dirt over each grave. It was strange to think such preparations were planned before the first shot was fired. Without a doubt, the military knew men would die and was prepared for it.

Upon arriving at the beach I had a tube inserted in my throat and a small vial of brandy poured into my body without benefit of taste. All corpsmen carried little bottles of brandy to help subdue shock. I received morphine, penicillin, and blood. Someone knelt down beside me and carefully began to cover my body with a poncho. It was alarming when it was pulled over my face. I thought to myself, *I'm dead and just don't know it!* Already struggling to breathe, I was concerned that covering my face would further impair my ability to inhale. The gunpowder and disturbed ash hung like a heavy cloud over the beach and the injured were covered to protect them from the elements. Slowly, the brandy and morphine began to take effect and I blissfully slipped into a glorious haze.

Night had closed on Iwo Jima and I was surrounded by darkness when the poncho was finally pulled off. Because of the risk of assault on our landing craft, the wounded were only taken out to the ships under cover of darkness. During the first few days of fighting, the numbers of wounded swelled beyond expectations. As a result, hundreds of the injured lay unattended for hours on Iwo's beaches.

Upon awakening, my senses were instantly assaulted with the pungency of gunpowder and death. Men all around me moaned, and waited in agony, for medical attention and evacuation. A northeast wind raged gale-force, whipping up a six-foot surf. My broken body was loaded onto an Amtrac and taken out to sea, eventually docking at a barge tied up to the LST I was to be transferred to. Sailors struggled in rough seas to move the injured from the Amtrac to the barge and once more from the barge to the LST. A huge swell washed over my barge, lifted my body up, and very nearly swept me overboard. Had it not been for a sailor who was quick to grab my leg, I would have been lost.

By crane, I was hoisted in a wire basket from the barge into the hold of an LST. As I was being lowered into the LST, I struggled to process what was taking place around me. I blinked several times to clear my vision and was totally unprepared for the sight that gradually came into focus. Everywhere I looked were hundreds of cots, each cradling the injured and dying bodies of American Marines. It was a heartbreaking sight to behold. These were America's finest young men and their lives were forever changed. As soon as more blood and medicine were administered to me, I was placed among them. As the morphine flowed through my veins, the pain began to ease. Eventually, I drifted off into the dark comfort of unconsciousness.

Time meant nothing to me. It was something I could only measure in the short spans of lucidity between morphine injections. When the lights were snapped on and off, I thought time was passing from day to night. I remember thinking I had been laying there for three days; in reality it was only one night.

It is hard to say how long I remained in the LST before I was loaded up, along with four or five other Marines, for transport to another ship. From the LST, I was placed on a Higgins boat and taken to a different vessel. They had no room for any more injured and I was turned away. On the return trip, the coxswain got lost in the choppy waters, which thrashed us about unmercifully, before he found his way back to the LST. This excursion had not only been a waste of time, but agonizing as well. My body was racked with pain and any movement was excruciating, not only for me, but the other injured as well.

The next day would involve a repeat of the day before, with additional misfortune. One more attempt was made to move me to another ship. This time I was to be placed aboard the hospital ship, *Samaritan*. As our Higgins boat came alongside the *Samaritan* in rough seas, a sailor attempted to drop a line to help steady our vessel so we could disembark. The sailor was patient in trying to exact the line down to our launch. An officer became irritated with the delay and took the rope from the sailor's hands. He lost his grip on the heavy coil and it plummeted forty-five feet from the ship's deck, slamming into my chest. The impact reopened my wounds and I exploded with pain. As if I had not bled enough already, dark crimson fluid poured from my body once again.

Another hospital ship stood vigilant off the shores of Iwo Jima, the *Solace*. In addition, some transport ships had been converted solely for medical purposes. The re-opening of my chest wounds, at the hands of the clumsy naval officer, made me a top priority. I was the first of our group to be taken aboard the hospital ship.

The doctor studied my shredded right arm and calculated the degree of damage. The look on his face was easy to interpret. In a consoling tone, he explained the mangled appendage would most likely need to be amputated. Just when I thought my circumstances could not get any worse, he delivered that disheartening blow. I had plans for that arm after I got out of service. Certain activities would require it to be functional. There were sports, school, hands to shake, cars to drive. Most importantly, I wanted to be able to wrap my arms around the girls back home—not one arm, but both—extended and wound tightly round those girls for long uninterrupted periods of time. My eyes, as well as my voice, pleaded with the surgeon, "Please save my arm. I don't really care what it looks like; just save it."

In a reassuring tone, the doctor said, "Son, I'll do the best I can." I was immediately put to sleep, not knowing if I would still have my arm when I woke up. I tried to count backward from one hundred, but my thoughts tended to drift. Though ambidextrous, my right arm was the one I depended on most. It baited my hooks, pitched baseball, and buttered my mother's homemade cornbread. I wondered what she was doing at that exact moment and tried to calculate the time differential. I have no memory of having ever completed the calculation.

While I floated in a chemically induced sleep, Marines continued their push toward the north end of the island. It would have been during this time Americans were fighting in the area known as Kuribayashi's "Meat Grinder." There were other killing grounds as well, a bowl-shaped area known as "The Amphitheater" and a craggy escarpment known as "Turkey Knob." Marines entering these zones met with withering fire from highly fortified enemy locations, capable of firing at the Americans from several different directions.

I had no idea how much time passed before I blinked awake and tried to sort out what had happened to me. For a moment, I wondered if it had all been a dream. Pain revisited every inch of my body and reality quickly caught up with me. Recalling my last memory of preparing for surgery, I slowly rolled my eyes downward and looked to see if I was still in one piece. I was.

The doctor explained to me that blood had coagulated with the volcanic ash in my wounds, providing a cast-like coating and protecting the limb to a certain extent. The force of the blast drove ash deep into my flesh, creating a sort of permanent tattooing. I would carry these souvenirs from Iwo with me for the rest of my life.

After surgery, maggots were placed into the wound and a proper plaster cast applied over the snacking herd of larvae. The young insects would devour only the rotten and dying flesh, increasing the probability of a better recovery. The movements of the maggots chewing on my arm nearly drove me crazy.

Ships were filled to capacity with wounded and Marines were being housed wherever space could be found. My quarters were above deck where I could hear more of what was happening than those below. Around midday on Friday, February 23, someone yelled excitedly, "Hey, they've raised the flag on Suribachi!" Ships blasted their horns in celebration and support of the troops, who still had their most intense fighting ahead of them. Everyone around me was pretty heavily medicated and unable to get in on the celebrating.

I was fortunate to have witnessed this marvelous event in American history. If my ship had been slightly port or starboard, or had I been placed in a different berth; if the door had been closed, or had I been heavily sedated, I might have missed it. However, I was able to look through the door and beyond the rail and see it in the distance. It was spectacular. Flying proudly 550 feet above the Pacific, for all the world to see, waved the most famous flag since Fort McHenry's stars and stripes inspired Francis Scott Key. From where I lay, it looked quite small, but it fluttered large in my heart. We had taken the high ground!

9

Torn and Shattered

We are determined that before the sun sets on this terrible struggle our flag will be recognized throughout the world as a symbol of freedom on the one hand, of overwhelming power on the other.

—George C. Marshall, Chief of Staff

I thought of my cousin, Sam, who was still on Iwo and hoped that he was all right. Sam's father, also named Sam, and my father were brothers. They were close in age, and according to family historians, you never saw one without the other. I had a strong attachment to my family. I viewed them as my most precious gift and treasured every memory of them.

When my father and Sam's father were little boys they loved to play in the woods. One evening, about dark, they dashed into their house, breathless with faces as white as ghosts. Their loving mother asked them, "What's the matter with you boys?" A wide-eyed Louis whispered, "Mama, listen. They're talking to each other." Sam nodded in agreement. Their mother stopped her meal preparation to listen. All she could hear were nighttime noises rising from the woods and over the pasture. "What are they saying?" she asked. My father said, "One of them said, 'Who's that?' and the other one said, 'Louis Lucas! Louis Lucas!' and 'Let's go get 'em. Let's go get 'em!'" Their mother did not want to make them feel foolish, so she did not laugh out loud. She carefully explained those were just hound dogs talking back and forth about something they heard in the woods and they had nothing to be afraid of. This was always one of my family's favorite stories.

NOW THE NEXT generation of Lucases had a story of our own to tell. Like our fathers, Sam and I had listened to the sounds of danger in the night. However, there was little comfort provided for us. I was confident that I would survive and hoped Sam would be as fortunate.

I wondered why Sam had not come to check on me while I was in the trench, since we were not very far from each other when the grenade detonated. I would find out six decades later why he had not. Sam Lucas was the relief BARman. When his team's BARman was killed, Sam had to replace him. Shortly thereafter, I encountered the grenades. When a Marine told Sam I had been injured, he wanted to find me. His sergeant told him that he and his Browning Automatic Rifle were needed to stay where they were emplaced and the request was denied. His orders were to "Hold the line!"

I would not leave Iwo's waters for several days after I was wounded. Hospital ships and ships transporting the wounded required destroyer escorts. Eventually, it was our turn and our convoy sailed en route to the nearest base hospital. Days later, our ship dropped anchor in Guam. The injured were transported by jeeps equipped with racks, capable of transporting four stretchers per vehicle. With three or four men assisting, I was loaded onto a rack and taken to the hospital. We traveled dirt roads that were deeply rutted by extensive use. The ride was not a pleasant one and men moaned in pain from being jostled about.

Night had fallen. Immediately upon arrival, I was assigned a bed in a ward that had a capacity of about thirty men. The following morning, medical staff proceeded to change my bandages. The extensive draining of grayish colored pus from my arm had soaked into the plaster cast until the entire dressing was a soggy mess. Two doctors came to remove it. As they carefully pried open the cast, I held my breath. So did everyone else. The foulness of the seepage was intolerable. The doctors departed immediately. Marines, recuperating in beds next to me, who thought they were immobile, crawled down the hall to escape the abhorrent stench. I could not get away from it and kept a pillow over my head to avoid the unpleasantness.

The medical personnel left me alone for a couple of hours, while the pus finished draining and the atmosphere cleared. When they returned, an examination was made of what remained of the appendage. As they carefully lifted my arm, the globs of gelatinous pus dripped from my elbow onto sterile white gauze that had been placed under the wound. As though looking through a chunk of

Swiss cheese, I could see daylight through the punctures in my flesh. After the maggots had completed their task, the flesh and muscle that remained was fresh and pink. I do not know what happened to the maggots; the smell alone should have killed them. My wound was flushed and cleansed. In an effort to prevent the outside of my arm healing before the inside had properly healed, all the holes were stuffed with gauze coated in petroleum jelly. Most of the damage was to my lower arm, leaving the Marine Corps tattoo on my upper bicep virtually unscathed.

The next few weeks of my life would see me through numerous surgeries, therapies, and convalescence. I had a lot of time to think about what had happened to me and why. I never felt that I would fail if given the opportunity to serve my country. It was my fate that these events should come to pass and it gave me great satisfaction that I was there when my friends needed me. Years before, I had an experience that left me with a sense of guilt that I had let a friend down, and it was painful for me. I never wanted to feel that way again. That good friend taught me a valuable lesson about the importance of taking care of each other. It was a lesson I would never forget.

At four years old, I was still an only child. One day, my father gave me a puppy. He thought puppies and boys went together and that they should watch over each other while both grew up. Skippy was a little Jack Russell terrier. He was solid white, but for a brown spot on his head. Wherever I went, Skippy went. We were real pals, Skippy and I.

One day, while living in the town of Plymouth, I went across the street to see a neighbor boy and Skippy went with me. We played little boy games while Skippy bounced around in the yard close by. As playtime ended, I crossed the street to return home. Noticing Skippy had remained in the neighbor's yard, I gave him a call, and upon hearing his master's voice, he obediently came running. I did not see the laundry truck coming down the street and the truck did not see the puppy. Skippy was not paying attention to anything but the sound of my voice. The driver could not stop in time and Skippy was killed instantly. Horrified, I screamed at the sight of losing my companion. A young man in his twenties stepped from behind the wheel of the truck and approached me. It had happened so quickly. He gently lifted Skippy's lifeless body and cradled it in his arms. After expressing his sorrow for the accident, he walked me home. I followed, trailing no more than a step behind, my eyes constantly shifting from Skippy's expressionless face to the ground. I looked away in an effort to hide my tears. My mother answered the front door, and upon seeing the motionless puppy, immediately began to cry. "I am so sorry, Mrs. Lucas," the driver said.

He placed Skippy on the back porch until my father got home to take care of matters. I had never experienced such a sense of loss. I watched Skippy for the longest time. He lay absolutely still. With all my heart, I tried to will him to open his eyes, wag his tail, and kiss my face once again. There was no going back, no reversal of the clock. It was over, the absolute and final end.

I was never told where he was buried. The guilt I felt for not having better protected my buddy weighed heavily on my heart. Every night, for the longest time, I cried myself to sleep over Skippy. I never had a better friend.

IN MARCH OF 1945, after a few weeks and several operations in the Guam Naval Hospital, I was placed aboard the transport, USS *Admiral C.F. Hughes*, and set sail for the United States. The walking wounded disembarked at Honolulu and the remainder of us continued on to San Francisco, where I received additional operations. I was near the end of my transit from Hawaii to California, when hostilities ended on Iwo Jima, March 26, 1945.

On March 21, Lieutenant Ronald B. Gittelsohn, USN, and a 5th Division chaplain assisted in the dedication of the 5th Marine Division Cemetery on Iwo Jima. Rabbi Ronald Gittelshon's poignant words have been compared to the Gettysburg Address. The lieutenant said

> Here before us lie the bodies of comrades and friends, men who until yesterday or last week, laughed with us, trained with us, men who were on the same ships with us, and went over the side with us as we prepared to hit the beaches of this island. Some of us have buried our closest friends here. We saw these men killed before our very eyes. Any one of us might have died in their place. Indeed some of us are alive and breathing at this very moment only because

men who lie here beneath us had the courage and strength to give their lives for ours.

These men have done their job well. They have paid the ghastly price of freedom. Here lie men who loved America because their ancestors, generations ago, helped in her founding because they themselves, or their own fathers, escaped from oppression to her blessed shores. Here lie officers and men, negroes and whites, rich men and poor—together. Theirs is the highest and purest democracy. Any man among us, the living, who fails to understand that will thereby betray those who lie here dead.

I was not there for the dedication and tribute to the fallen, but I did not need to be. Everything that was said I already knew. I would never forget.

My stay in San Francisco was short, only six days, but it was long enough for twenty dollars in emergency pay to catch up with me on March 30. Since the time I was separated from my pack and wallet, I had been without funds.

On April 3, 1945, along with other wounded, I was transported by troop train from San Francisco to a naval hospital in Charleston, South Carolina. The trip back to the Carolinas seemed different than the one that I had taken coming out to San Diego almost two years before. Perhaps the trip itself was not different; maybe it was me. I had always loved my country dearly, but after Iwo Jima, I possessed a much deeper appreciation for her. In addition, my pride in the Corps had more deeply rooted itself in my heart and I knew it would remain with me forever. An enormous price was being paid to guarantee our liberty. I had seen it with my own eyes and personally made payment in more units of blood than I could count. No matter the cost, she was well worth fighting for.

Through the train's windows, I savored scenes of my wonderful country stretching out as far as the eye could see, mile after glorious mile of the most beautiful land on earth. In my head the phrases repeated themselves over and over, like a broken record, *Oh beautiful, for spacious skies, for amber waves of grain.* There was never any doubt in my mind I had made the right decision, to take control of my own destiny. I loved this land and I wanted to protect her from those who would do her harm. *For purple mountain majesties, above the fruited plain.* I had done my little part to keep her safe and in the hands of those who loved her best. I shut my eyes and thanked God for all His blessings, and prayed He would continue to "shed His grace" on her, and on me.

Two days out from my destination, history turned a corner. In a small white clapboard house in Georgia, known as "The Little White House," President Roosevelt relaxed in a leather armchair for a visit with a handful of family and friends. After having lighted a cigarette, the president reached up, touched his temple and suddenly dropped his hand. It was 1315 hours. Having suffered a cerebral hemorrhage, the president lingered unconscious for another two hours and twenty minutes before his heart beat for the last time.

On April 14, 1945, two days after the death of President Franklin D. Roosevelt, I, along with other wounded, arrived in Charleston, the end of the line for the cross-country troop train. We were met by nurses and transported to a hospital where doctors removed numerous pieces of shrapnel from my body. However, eight pieces would remain in my brain, six in my right lung, and over a hundred more throughout my body. Nurses took care of all my needs until I was able to handle them on my own. I had to learn to take care of myself, to bathe, dress, write, and brush my teeth, all with my left hand. Every day hospital staff took me to therapy and assisted me in learning to walk again. It was painful and exhausting.

As I endured each difficult session, I thought of my

brother, Louis Ed, and how I helped him learn to walk again after an accident.

Louis Ed was just a young child when struck by a car while riding his bike down Main Street in Belhaven, North Carolina. The driver helped Louis Ed to his car and drove him home. A doctor examined my brother and determined there was nothing seriously wrong with him.

As time passed Louis began to develop signs he had sustained a more serious injury than first thought. An additional examination revealed his hip had been knocked from its socket. In order to correct the problem, Louis had to wear a full body cast. My poor brother lay on his back for eighteen months while the injury mended. He never complained, though his cast had to be replaced four times. Family members removed the final cast after Louis developed sores and suffered so much physical discomfort that they determined he needed immediate relief.

It was four long months before he would ever walk again. I tried to aid in the long slow process of restoring his strength and mobility.

When I came home on leave, I would hold him under his arms and help him regain the use of his legs. His frame was smaller and more fragile than mine, and it gave me great pleasure to share my strength with a brother who meant so much to me.

The military did its part to restore the health and strength of the injured. Steak was served at nearly every meal. I received the very best care.

I recall great jubilation in the hospital when President Harry Truman announced Germany's surrender May 8, 1945. He expressed to the American people his sorrow that President Roosevelt did not live to witness the flags of freedom flying over Europe. I was in no condition to participate in the revelry, but my heart filled with renewed hope that hostilities in the Pacific would end soon, allowing Americans serving in the Armed Forces to return home to their loved ones.

In early summer I was allowed to go home for a few days. My mother had received a telegram many months before which informed her of my injuries. The telegram had failed to disclose any information as to where I was injured or the degree of my injuries. She only knew I was not dead, not yet. I took the train from Charleston to North Carolina. I knew I was nearing home when I spied fields being prepared for a new tobacco crop. For the last three years, every time I caught the scent of a freshly lit cigarette it reminded me of Carolina tobacco fields and home.

I was delighted to be back in North Carolina. The hometown girls went out of their way to give me a proper welcome. I cautioned them to please be gentle with me; after all, I was a wounded boy. Everyone showered me with love and affection. It was wonderful. My mom bought me a blue 1936 Ford coupe. It was a manual shift, and with my useless right arm, I had to steer and shift left-handed. I was pretty good at it too.

I returned to Charleston around June to continue my convalescence. Each day I worked with a physical therapist to try and regain as much use of my limbs as possible. The daily routine hardly afforded me the level of recreation I desired. In search of much livelier entertainment, I slipped out through a hole in the fence one night and caught a ride to a bar.

I had no identification and no money. Generally easygoing and loquacious by nature, I made friends easily. It was not long before two Marines started buying me drinks and I was content while the drinks kept coming. As can sometimes happen in a bar, my new Marine friends started arguing. They stopped spending money and that irritated me. One thing led to another and I hit one guy with my left fist before I was struck in the head with a bottle. Blood trickled from the gash, but it did not faze me. People around the bar were stunned that I did not react to the blow. The bartender called the Shore Patrol while a Marine hustled me out of the bar and back to the Navy Yard. The guard on duty let me through the gate without reporting me. The Marine that took me back to camp also took me to the dispensary where my head wound was closed with eight stitches. I went to sleep without ever seeing what I looked like. The following morning I was startled when I went to shave and saw the strange-looking man in a white turban staring back at me from the mirror.

By early fall I was living in the casualty barracks a hundred yards away from the hospital. I would remain there until receiving a medical discharge from the service on September 18, 1945. My recuperation period was drawing to a close; so was Japan's dominance of the East.

Anyone that read a newspaper or watched a newsreel knew that the United States was island hopping across the Pacific, like skipping stones across a creek, for the eventual invasion of Japan. It was also a well-known fact that the Japanese people were indoctrinated to fight to the death if necessary to repel an invasion of their mainland. There would be considerable loss of life on both sides.

The responsibility of giving the final nod to drop the bomb rested solely on President Truman's shoulders. Following the recommendation of his advisors. Truman agreed the bomb should be dropped as soon as possible and with no warning. It was a decision with which I strongly agreed.

With several possible target cities available, the United States did not make the final decision until the B-29s reached the island of Japan. As a gray undercast covered most of Japan, the clouds opened up over Hiroshima exposing her to the flight crew of the Enola Gay, as though fate had marked her for destruction. One hundred fifty thousand Japanese lost their lives as a result. Though miles off its target due to poor visibility, the second bomb dropped on Nagasaki three days later killed seventy-five thousand more.

Hostilities ended between Japan and the Allied nations on August 14, 1945, when Japan agreed to an unconditional surrender. The official Victory Over Japan Day is August 15. The surrender was later made formal on September 2, aboard the USS *Missouri* in Tokyo Bay. At last, the most devastating war in human history was over. We cheered, elated at the prospect of an end to the killing, and resuming a normal life in postwar America.

Before receiving my discharge from the hospital, I heard I was to receive some sort of medal, but I did not know what. I knew very little about medals, having never studied them. I did not fight the Japanese for medals, only to serve the country I loved. Though I had no knowledge of it at the time, the battalion adjutant, Lieutenant Gene Hochfelder, wrote a recommendation for me to be awarded the Navy Cross for my action on Iwo Jima.

As the administrative officer aboard the USS *Deuel*, Lieutenant Hochfelder was responsible for personnel matters. Thus, stowaways were his department. During wartime, a stowaway was a very serious matter. In years to come, Gene Hochfelder would share with me his thoughts upon meeting me for the first time. He said, "You were a personable, baby-faced kid, full of piss and vinegar." He further reflected, "As the time of the beach landing grew near, the seemingly tougher Marines had a hard time with what was about to happen. Some of the smaller guys surprised us with their tough and ready attitude. 'Tough and ready,' that was you, Jack."

On September 18, 1945, physically unfit for duty, I was discharged from service and went home to Belhaven, North Carolina, twenty-two pounds lighter and two and three-quarter inches shorter than when I first left. My girlfriend, Carolyn Brown, came down from Portsmouth and I met her at the bus station with a passionate, glad-to-be-home kiss. We both stayed in Plymouth to be close to one another. She stayed with friends and I with my aunt, Mittie Edwards Blackman. We visited a great deal over the next few days. I had loved Carolyn since we were children. She had the most gorgeous head of hair. I remember the first time I saw her. Her hair bounced with every step she took and so did my heart. There was never any question that Carolyn was the girl for me.

I had been in Plymouth for about a week when my mother received a call from Washington, DC. The caller asked where I could be reached. She gave the caller the telephone number at my aunt Mittie's house. My mother instructed me to be available at a specific time to receive an important call. The president of the United States had a message for me.

At some point in the afternoon, the phone rang at Aunt Mittie's. It was the White House. Someone was calling on behalf of President Truman to tell me to be in Washington, DC, on October 2, 1945. I had not misunderstood the reason for the call. The message was clear; I was to be decorated with the nation's highest award for valor, the Medal of Honor.

10

The Fightin'est Marine

No person was ever honored for what he received; honor has been the reward for what he gave.

—President Calvin Coolidge

Legislation dictates no margin of error when determining whether a member of the armed forces is entitled to the Medal of Honor. The deed must be

proven, by incontestable evidence, of at least two eyewitnesses; it must be so outstanding, that it clearly distinguished his gallantry, beyond the call of duty from lesser forms of bravery; it must involve the risk of his life; it must be the type of deed which, if he had not done it, would not subject him to any justified criticism.

I asked my friend, Lloyd McNair, to go along with me on the all-expense-paid trip to Washington, and he agreed. He was a good companion. Lloyd was one year ahead of me in school and we had a great deal in common. He loved to drink hard, drive fast, and chase women. On October 2, 1945, my friend and I boarded a train in North Carolina and headed north. My family decided to come up a day later than us.

Lloyd and I propped our feet up, pulled our hats down over our eyes, and slumped down in the seats for the trip. I tried, but could not sleep. Perhaps it was all the excitement, or more likely, Lloyd's incessant snoring. The boy could always sleep anywhere. The train stopped at an old Virginia rail station. With green siding, a dark-red tin roof and cobblestone pavement, the depot had a classic appearance, like a Norman Rockwell painting. On the platform stood a young woman holding the hand of a small child. She was pretty, in a plain sort of way, wearing a look of anticipation, as though she was waiting on someone. I looked at the child, a little boy, maybe four years old. He was far too young to understand the events that had taken place around him, events that would determine his future as well as everyone else's. The world had changed a great deal in his short lifetime. As a result, he would remain free to decide his profession, free to choose his religion, and free to speak his mind. I hoped his young eyes would never witness the horrors that mine had.

A Marine threw his sea bag from the train onto the platform. With both hands, he clutched the stairs' railing tightly, and with some difficulty, he stepped down to the platform and stood rather shakily while the conductor handed him his cane. The woman rushed forward, quickly closing the space between them and knocking the cane from his grip. The Marine stumbled a little but the woman held him steady in her firm embrace. The little boy looked up at the couple and tugged several times at the Marine's pants' leg. The man released the woman from one arm, for only as long as it took to scoop the young boy up to join them in a three-way embrace. Friends came forward and gathered around the family. The air was full of happy and excited voices. The soldier leaned heavily on the shoulders of others who gladly supported him as they headed for home. A man carried the Marine's sea bag for him and the little boy trailed behind waving the abandoned cane in the air. The Marine was fortunate, no matter the degree of his injuries. He came home alive to the people who loved him.

The train set off again and eventually pulled into Union Station. Lloyd and I caught a cab and headed for our hotel in downtown Washington, DC. Wanting to look my best, I had taken great pains in polishing the leather brim of my Marine dress cover. I treasured that cap. While climbing into the cab, I placed it under the back window for safekeeping. Washington, DC, was beautiful and I marveled at the buildings, monuments, and big-city activity. In all the excitement, I forgot my cap when I exited the cab. I never saw it again.

Immediately upon my arrival at the hotel, reporters began calling, attempting to line up interviews with me. I was amazed at all the fuss everyone was making over me; so was Lloyd. I checked into the nice hotel room and dropped my body onto the sofa with a thud. I bounced on the seat cushions a couple of times, put my feet up on the coffee table, and laid my head back in my palms. Lloyd, still trying to take it all in, let out a long whistle in amazement. I told him, "All this attention is going to take a little getting used to, but I'll manage." He shook his head in disbelief. I added, "By the way, Lloyd, if you need anything, just tell them you're with me." Lloyd picked up a pillow from a chair and threw it at me. I said, "Hey! Watch it; that's probably pure silk. If you're going to hang out with somebody famous like me, you need to learn how to act." He threw another pillow. Yes sir, life was good.

The excitement of the trip began to take its toll; I was ready for some shut-eye. I crawled between the crisp clean hotel sheets and figured I would drop off as soon as my head hit the pillow. I did not. Something was nagging at me and I could not put it out of my mind. I deeply appreciated being recognized for my deed on Iwo Jima. I knew my country was doing all she could to demonstrate how much my actions meant to her. However, every time I shut my eyes, images of Iwo Jima flashed in my head. The bodies of dead Marines on the beach, and rows of stretchers bearing the dead and dying would forever be with me. I saw their faces and I grieved for them and their families.

The act for which I was to receive the medal was not an exclusive one; other Marines had covered live grenades with their bodies during the battle for Iwo Jima. However, their medals would be presented to their next of kin. They would never hear the applause or shake the president's hand. Girls would never kiss them in parades. Most importantly, they would never experience the thrill of having the inverted star, hanging from the blue satin ribbon, fastened around their neck.

I wondered how many other extraordinary acts of heroism went unseen and thus unreported. I was honored, yet humbled. Other Americans' acts of bravery would go unsung, while mine would not. I made up my mind, right then and there; I would not only wear the medal to represent my action, but also to honor the spirit of those other brave men who were not as fortunate as I. I had faith that God, in His infinite wisdom, was rewarding them for the price they paid in far greater measure than could ever be extended them on earth. I had to believe that; it was the only way I could make peace with their sacrifice.

The following morning, October 3, my mother came to Washington, DC, and brought my brother, stepfather, stepbrother, and my girlfriend. I noticed as soon as I saw Louis Ed's black eye that he was keeping the Lucas legacy alive and well, having fought a battle of his own back in North Carolina. I laughed and put my arm around him when I saw it. The battle-scarred little brother was a detail the newspapers quickly picked up on and reported with a reference to the eleven-year-old's "fighting decoration." These days were filled with wonder for us all.

First thing that morning, I met with Margaret Kernodle, a reporter from the Associated Press, for a pancake breakfast. She immediately began asking me questions about the fighting convictions and confinements to the brig listed on my military records. I never intended to divulge that information and was stunned journalists had already examined my history. I probably should not have been so surprised because I had received a lot of press coverage as the youngest Marine recipient of the Medal of Honor. During this same time, Gregory "Pappy" Boyington was being touted as the top Marine ace of World War II. My family and friends were proud and that mattered more than any press coverage. Still, all the attention was beginning to go to my head a little.

I heard that every major newspaper was carrying my story and I wanted to read what was being written about me. In the Associated Press article, I made a request of the American people. I said, "I sure hope all you folks will send me newspaper clippings about myself," and I gave my mother's mailing address. Flying high on a national wave of attention, I mused with another reporter, "As soon as I rest up some, I'll probably run for president." Following breakfast, Ms. Kernodle took my girlfriend and me to the newspaper office to show us around. We watched as our photo rotated on a cylindrical apparatus that sent our images nationwide over the wire. The next day's *Washington Post* headline read, "The Fightin'est Marine."

On the morning of October 4, 1945, recipients were picked up from the hotel and transported to Marine headquarters, near Arlington, Virginia. A photographer was there to take our official Marine Corps photos. I still had my uniform. Anyone being discharged from service could continue to wear the uniform for ninety days; a Medal of Honor recipient could wear it any time.

There were several people at the headquarters to assist. They hurried about trying to locate a hat for me, to replace the one I left in the cab. Unable to find a dress cover like the one I lost, I had to settle for a "piss cutter" type. I needed a size seven and one-half, but a seven and one-quarter was all that could be found. Because it was a size too small, it did not fit my head correctly and I had to cock it at a funny angle just to keep it on.

We lined up for our photos. A duplicate Medal of Honor, used by the Marine Corps only in these official photo shoots, was placed around the neck of a recipient. After a photo was taken, the medal was removed and used again for the next recipient's photo. The actual medal would be presented later.

Following the taking of photographs, Marine recipients assembled in the office of General Alexander Vandergrift, the commandant of the Marine Corps. The ceremony was brief, but its purpose served. We watched respectfully as Colonel Pappy Boyington, fresh from a Japanese prisoner of war camp, was presented with the Navy Cross. Pappy's service to his country would be well publicized in the years to follow.

I liked being among Marines. They had been my family and I thought of each of them as brothers. It was a wonderful day, preparing for the proudest moment of my life, and I had thoroughly enjoyed every minute of it.

Morning dawned beautiful on October 5. The day was completely perfect. Recipients, along with their families, were shuttled to the White House for the medal presentations. The United States Navy Band, military personnel, dignitaries, and honored guests formed on the South Lawn of the White House with the president. The grounds were shipshape and everyone was seated in his respective section for the ceremony. Recipients of the medal sat as a group, closest to the president. I took my place in the middle of the second row of the fourteen recipients. The bright sun glistening off the polished Navy Band instruments was blinding and my bright smile blinded them right back. All the big brass from every branch of the service were in attendance, as well as members of Congress and the president's Cabinet.

Instead of sitting with the dignitaries, General George Marshall joined my family and sat with my mother. There were music, speeches, and smiles all around. A gentle breeze blew warm across a crystal-blue coastal sky, but it was not enough to prevent three members of the Marine Guard of Honor from fainting during the forty-minute ceremony, battle fatigue still evident on their faces. First aid was immediately rendered and they rejoined their ranks.

Vice Admiral Louis E. Denfeld, chief of navy personnel, began announcing the names of the recipients and reading their citations. President Truman was visibly moved when Sergeant William G. Harrell, a twenty-three-year-old from Texas, stepped forward to face the chief executive and snapped a salute. He wore hooks where he once had hands. The president hung the medal around the sergeant's neck and warmly shook his arm at the elbow.

The moment had arrived; my name was announced, "Private First Class, Jack H. Lucas, United States Marine Corps." As I rose and made my way to the podium, I drew in deep breaths to keep my head clear. I wanted to be able to commit every detail of this moment to memory. I faced the president as he carefully removed the Medal of Honor from its box and placed the blue ribbon, adorned with thirteen small white stars, around my neck. I was receiving the nation's highest recognition for valor; my heart nearly burst with pride. When President Truman initially greeted me, he grabbed my right forearm with his left hand and inadvertently stuck his fingers into my wound. It hurt, but I managed not to wince. The small hat I had been issued was sitting precariously atop my head. When he shook my hand, he pumped my arm so hard he nearly shook my hat off. It would not have mattered if he had. Nothing could have spoiled this day for me. I was absolutely delighted to be recognized by my nation and even more so at having served her so well. President Truman said, "I would rather have this medal than be president of the United States." I replied, "Sir, I'll swap ya'!" He laughed and moved me along.

In closing the ceremony President Truman said, "We have won two great victories and we face another fight, a fight for a peaceful world. This fight for peace is necessary, so we won't have to go to war again, so we won't have to maim the flower of our young men and bury them. Now let us go forward and win that fight, as we have won these two victories, and this war will not have been in vain."

As the president spoke, I closed my eyes and breathed in the fresh clean air of freedom. A slight grin bent the corners of my mouth. Marines were being decorated on this day, not killed. It was a great day for me, my family, America, and the Corps.

11

The Medal of Honor

I am certain that after the dust of centuries has
passed over our cities, we, too, will be remembered not for victories or defeats in battle or in
politics, but for our contribution to the human
spirit.

—President John F. Kennedy

The citation read

For conspicuous gallantry and intrepidity at
the risk of his life above and beyond the call of
duty while serving with the 1st Battalion, 26th
Marines, 5th Marine Division, during action

against enemy forces on Iwo Jima, Volcano Islands, 20 February 1945. While creeping through a treacherous, twisting ravine, which ran in close proximity to a fluid and uncertain frontline on D-plus-1 day, Pfc. Lucas and 3 other men were suddenly ambushed by a hostile patrol, which savagely attacked with rifle fire and grenades. Quick to act when the lives of the small group were endangered by 2 grenades which landed directly in front of them, Pfc. Lucas unhesitatingly hurled himself over his comrades upon 1 grenade and pulled the other under him, absorbing the whole blasting forces of the explosions in his own body in order to shield his companions from the concussion and murderous flying fragments. By his inspiring action and valiant spirit of self-sacrifice, he not only protected his comrades from certain injury or possible death but also enabled them to rout the Japanese patrol and continue the advance. His exceptionally courageous initiative and loyalty reflect the highest credit upon Pfc. Lucas and the U.S. Naval Service.

(At the time the citation was written, it was not clear to officials whether or not the second grenade had detonated. However, as far as qualifying for the Medal of Honor was concerned, it made no difference.)

CAPTAIN DUNLAP, TO whom I surrendered aboard the USS *Deuel*, had recommended me for the Medal of Honor. At the time I was decorated, he was in the hospital recovering from a hip wound he suffered on Iwo Jima. He would receive his own Medal of Honor from President Truman on December 18, 1945.

I was in good company the day of my decoration. There were fourteen recipients, including myself:

Lieutenant Colonel Gregory "Pappy" Boyington,
   age 32, Okanogan, Washington;
Commander George Levick Street, III, age 32,
   Norfolk, Virginia;
Major Louis H. Wilson, Jr., age 25, Brandon,
   Mississippi;
Captain Joseph J. McCarthy, age 34, Ironwood,
   Michigan;

Second Lieutenant Arthur Junior Jackson, age 20,
Portland, Oregon;
Sergeant William G. Harrell, age 23, Mercedes,
Texas;
Pharmacist's Mate George E. Wahlen, age 21,
Ogden, Utah;
Hospital Apprentice Robert E. Bush, age 19,
Tacoma, Washington;
Corporal Richard E. Bush, age 21, Glasgow,
Kentucky;
Corporal Douglas T. Jacobson, age 20, Port
Washington, New York;
Corporal Hershel Woodrow "Woody" Williams,
age 22, Fairmont, West Virginia;
Private Franklin E. Sigler, age 20, Little Falls,
New Jersey;
Private Wilson D. Watson, age 24, Earl, Arkansas

Following the ceremony, recipients, along with Admiral
Chester Nimitz, participated in a parade down Pennsylvania Avenue. We sat four or five to a vehicle, following the car carrying Admiral Nimitz. Motorcycle escorts
flanked the admiral's car. Huge crowds lined both sides
of the street and cheered us along the way. Women rushed
up to our cars to touch us. Children waved small Amer-

ican flags. The young, the old, the tall, and the small turned out en masse to congratulate us; it was fabulous. Our procession ended at the Capitol where officials directed us inside. Upon entering the House Chamber, we were greeted with a standing ovation by House and Senate members. Admiral Nimitz spoke to the body, which was appropriate, for this day had been proclaimed Admiral Nimitz Day.

One of the day's spectacular events included watching a parade from reviewing stands assembled on the Washington Monument grounds. Recipients were permitted to have a guest attend with them; I chose my mother. It was a grand experience for a young kid from North Carolina and this was just the beginning.

In the evening, recipients and their families were entertained at a spectacular gala at the Mayflower Hotel in downtown Washington, DC. I met General Marshall, commander of the army; Admiral Ernest J. King, commander over all naval forces; Admiral Nimitz, commander over all naval forces in the Pacific; General Holland M. "Howlin' Mad" Smith, commander of forces at Iwo Jima; and Secretary of the Navy James Forrestal. I was privileged to talk to General Marshall for about half an hour that evening. It impressed me that he would take the time to speak with my girlfriend and me. Eddie Duchin, the famous pianist and band leader, played the piano. The night was unbelievable, an evening full of glitz, glamour, diamond rings, big shots, and immense wealth and power. My big day in DC was at an end, but there was still more excitement to come.

On October 7, Admiral King had me flown, along with other recipients of the Medal of Honor, to New York City. Admiral Nimitz flew up on his own plane. New York had rolled out the proverbial red carpet for us. At the airport, we were welcomed by Mayor Fiorello LaGuardia. Immediately upon arrival, the press began snapping pictures of Nimitz and me. It seemed everywhere I went, flashbulbs popped and people wanted to shake my hand and get an autograph.

Fifth Avenue welcomed us with all the pomp and fanfare that traditionally accompanies a New York ticker tape parade. Lining both sides of the street, the crowd was three-million strong. I waved at the women in the office windows and blew them kisses. As I rode along in a car behind Admiral Nimitz, a young girl broke out of the crowd, grabbed me tightly, and kissed me. She was pretty, but what I remember most was the kiss. I had never had a woman throw herself at me before and found it unbelievable. I liked it. I would never again be without a woman's companionship. Females would prove to always be my weakness. I had a real eye for the ladies. They were wonderful. I loved them all.

The parade progressed to City Hall where Admiral Nimitz was honored and presented with a gold medal by Mayor LaGuardia. Weeks later, Admiral Nimitz had duplicate medals struck in silver, otherwise identical to his own. He sent one to each of the Medal of Honor recipients who had accompanied him to New York City. In addition, each of us received a letter of thanks for our contribution to the war effort.

After the parade, we were served lunch at the Skylight Roof dining room at the Waldorf Astoria Hotel. Admiral Nimitz and I were seated at a table that accommodated twenty people. I was furnished a model as an escort. She was tall, blonde, and beautiful. When the music started, she and I danced all around the room. Perhaps I was not supposed to, but I did. Having this gorgeous woman in my arms eased my usual broad smile into bursts of laughter. I reveled in the sheer joy of just being alive.

That evening, the other special guests and I were treated to a magnificent banquet. We dined with the elite; Governor Thomas E. Dewey and the Rockefellers were in attendance. Entertainment included radio star and ventriloquist Edgar Bergen and his dummy Charlie McCarthy. (Six months later Edgar's daughter, Candice Bergen would be born.) It was on this occasion that I tasted my first caviar. Heaped in a small crystal dish beside my plate, the delicacy looked like little dark blueberries. I asked, "What is this?" Someone said, "It's caviar; try it!" I spooned some into my mouth and swallowed. I didn't think it was fit for crab bait.

I checked into a plush suite with white carpet about three inches thick and the tall beautiful model checked in with me. Surrounded by all this glitz and glamour, it was easy to forget about the girlfriend I'd left back home. The model and I partied with great enthusiasm all night long. The next morning, I was supposed to be on Kate Smith's radio show, but I was too exhausted to go. I called her and apologized for the cancellation as politely as possible.

My life would continue to be a series of public appearances. I was amazed and thrilled by all the attention. I was asked to travel many miles and appear at many events. Like a celebrity, I participated in the War Bond Drive. Wars are expensive and America still had a great debt to pay.

After receiving the Medal of Honor, my service record was cleared, and though I had worked hard to attain those seventeen convictions, every last one was expunged. The Medal of Honor opened many doors for me all the rest of my days, taking me almost anywhere I wanted to go.

12

Fulfilling a Promise

A man who has never gone to school may steal
from a freight car, but if he has a university education, he may steal the whole railroad.
                                    —President Franklin D. Roosevelt

The public request I had made to "send me newspaper clippings about myself" began to bear fruit. That
simple appeal generated a deluge of over fifty thousand
letters, eventually flooding the small Belhaven, North
Carolina, post office. My mother took five huge wash-
tubs downtown to the postmaster. Once they were filled
to capacity with letters, the mailman delivered them to
our house. I received love letters by the thousands and

countless envelopes containing money. This windfall enabled me to purchase a building lot in Plymouth, in one of the town's nicest sections. Eventually, a local car dealer wanted to buy it and offered me a brand-new Chevrolet in exchange. If women were my first love in life, cars ran a very close second, thus the deal was struck.

I attended many gatherings of Medal of Honor recipients. During one event, not long after I was decorated, another Medal of Honor recipient challenged me to see who was the toughest. On this occasion, the challenger was a friend of mine and all our horsing around was in fun. I turned him upside down and stamped his shoe-prints on the ceiling. Unfortunately, in the process of flipping my friend upside down, I split my pants, the only pair I had with me. To make matters worse, I had to fly to DC afterward on a general's plane with a split seat. Thankfully, I was wearing my green undershorts, which blended well with my green pants.

It was a bright time in my life. I loved seeing my picture in various publications and newsreels. However, not all news was good. Sadly, shocking details of the Holocaust and the ongoing suffering of humanity in Europe were unfolding. The war crimes' tribunal, known as the Nuremberg Trial, had begun in Germany. It lasted from

October 1945 until October 1946. The convicted were executed, and ironically, their bodies were transported to Dachau Concentration Camp to be cremated in crematoriums of their own making.

There was a similar international military tribunal for Japanese war criminals, but it drew less interest than the one in Nuremberg, Germany. Over a period of three years, a total of twenty-five high-ranking Japanese officers were tried. The most famous of the accused was Japan's chief of Japanese Army general staff and military dictator, Hideki Tojo, Japan's equivalent to Adolf Hitler. In the end, Tojo and six others were sentenced to death by hanging. Another sixteen criminals were sentenced to life in prison. Other Far East nations conducted their own trials which resulted in the death sentences of an additional nine hundred military officials.

While the rest of the world was tending to the details of rebuilding countries and lives, I realized it was time for me to think of my future as well. In 1945, the American Legion invited a number of Medal of Honor recipients to Chicago. There I met Chester R. Davis, vice president of Chicago Title and Trust Company and a University of Illinois board member. He asked if I would consider attending school in Illinois. The school wanted the publicity and I needed an education. In keeping the promise I made to my mother, I enrolled in a special high school program for veterans at the University of Illinois at Champaign. I was determined to complete my education.

In early 1946, I left home en route to Illinois in my new black Chevrolet. On my first trip to Champaign, I ran into a snowstorm. Flakes were showering so hard I could not see where I was going and was forced to pull over and stop for the night beside an old service station. I slept, huddled tightly in my car, all night long. I do not remember having ever been so cold.

Chilled to the bone, I awoke many times and wrapped my covers around me as tightly as possible before dozing off once again. Since I could not sleep soundly, I dreamt off and on throughout the seemingly endless night. Back home, they called this kind of cold "good hog-killing weather." In the old days, there was no refrigeration, thus a hog was killed during the time of year when there were enough successive cold days to process the meat without spoilage.

I reminisced about warmer nights. Winter's fury raged and a gust of arctic wind punched my car, its force rocking the vehicle back and forth, returning my thoughts to the cold, harsh reality of a Midwest winter. The night was long, cold, lonely, and miserable beyond measure.

Once I arrived in Champaign, I moved in with Professor Harnish and his family and began my high school curriculum. There was quite a lot of attention given me at the university. Everyone treated me like a celebrity. The professor's wife kept many newspaper articles about me and presented them to me years later, shortly before she died at the age of 104. The young ladies loved me and life was good. After all, I was the only seventeen-year-old high school freshman in America driving a new car and wearing the Medal of Honor. So many women, so little time.

Fate had placed me in an excellent position to meet many important people. Had I been smart and taken advantage of my opportunities, my success in life would have been limited only by my imagination. However, I had been burning up the roads between Illinois and North Carolina to see my girlfriend back home. Eventually, my heart won over my education. The president of the university pleaded with me to stay, but I returned east and began attending Maury High School in Norfolk, Virginia, to be closer to my sweetheart. Since I was allowed to pursue my high school diploma at my own pace, I moved through my studies with relative quickness, requiring assistance only when it came to advanced mathematics.

My school year was sometimes interrupted with various Medal of Honor events. In 1946, the American Legion treated me to a trip to San Francisco. They put me up at the Saint Francis Hotel. Medal of Honor recipients and special guests were entertained at the event by Bob Hope and Jerry Colonna. Needless to say, no other high school students were there. One evening, while dining at the Millionaires Club, actor Morton Downey approached me and suggested I allow him to take me to Hollywood and try my hand at acting. This was before Audie Murphy accepted a similar proposal by James Cagney. I should have accepted, but I was unable to break emotional ties to the girl I'd have to leave behind.

During this period in my life I lacked direction and—in my girlfriend's family's opinion—potential and height. Her parents were not looking for a son-in-law. They discouraged our relationship. Ultimately, my girlfriend began to see things their way and left me. It broke my heart. I had other issues I was dealing with as well. My sleep was haunted by horrifying images of planes flying overhead, strafing bullets, and explosions going off all around me. There was no logical explanation for the nightmare as I'd never been in that particular setting in reality. I attended counseling sessions until my psychologist committed suicide. At that point I figured I was more sound than they were and was better off dealing with my problems on my own.

At President Truman's request, I was offered employment in Winston-Salem, North Carolina, as a Veterans Administration (VA) representative. I accepted and my duties were scheduled so that I worked in the morning and attended the local R.J. Reynolds High School in the afternoon.

I graduated in a year and a half. Following graduation, I took a leave of absence from the VA and enrolled in Duke University, in Durham, North Carolina, on the GI Bill. School was challenging, since I had not yet been diagnosed with permanent hearing loss. I sat on the front row in all my classes in a constant struggle to hear what my professors were saying over the continuous ringing in my ears. Once the impairment was diagnosed, I was fitted for hearing aids and at least one obstacle in my life was conquered.

I had some great roommates at Duke that would turn out to be lifelong friends: Byrd Looper, Jimmy Spencer, and Pete Huffstickler. I never told anyone at Duke about my Medal of Honor. My roommates knew I was a Marine Corps veteran, but they had no knowledge of the medal. One afternoon there was a knock at our door. A reporter from the *Durham Morning Herald* wanted to interview me about my action on Iwo Jima and subsequent decoration. I consented. As my roommates looked on, I pulled out my footlocker. Everyone's eyes widened when I opened the lid and revealed an eight-by-ten glossy of Truman placing the Medal of Honor around my neck. Lying atop the photo was the actual Medal of Honor. As I told my story, all mouths were agape in astonishment. I had done a good job keeping it a secret, but now the news was out. I became an instant campus celebrity, but I managed to take it all in stride.

I developed a reputation around campus for a quick temper. Once, the drink machines were taking money and not giving drinks. I got really upset about it, lost my cool, and began shaking the machine violently, kicking and hitting it until I tired. I did not tire easily. Another time, some international students thought it amusing to drop water bombs from their third-floor window to unwary passersby. I never liked being bombed by anything, be it live mortars or plastic bags of water. Skipping every other step up the stairwell, I made my way to the perpetrators' room. I kicked open the door, grabbed a couple of the guys, and made it clear their behavior was not appreciated. There were no more water bomb incidents after that.

Byrd and Pete played on the football team. Every afternoon they came back to our room after practice, relaying how tough it was. I told them I was as tough as anybody and would like to give it a try. They told me the coaches might let me walk on, if I really wanted to give it a shot. I accepted. The next day, I showed up in the dressing room, suited up in heavy practice gear, and walked onto the field.

It was my assignment to hold a padded blocking shield for the Duke linemen who delivered vicious blows. One after another, they gave me all they had to see just how tough the "war hero" really was. They were not disappointed. Unfortunately, their hits were not always on target and my injured arm was taking a bashing. The old grenade wounds started opening up and bleeding. The trainer advised me it would not be in my best interest to pursue football. The risk was too great. My body could never contain my spirit which was always stronger than flesh and bone.

In the spring of 1950, during my second year at Duke, I received a letter from the Marine Corps that my personal effects were being returned to me. Enclosed with the letter was a check from the United States government for sixteen dollars, the exact amount I had in my wallet when I was injured. Apparently, the military collected the personal effects left scattered on the battlefield and stored them for their eventual return to the proper owner. When the bundle arrived, I opened it immediately, and found my wallet. Still inside were my pictures, the note to my mother written on a piece of ammo box cardboard, and all the Japanese souvenirs I had collected on the island. The return of my property was not only indicative of the Marine Corps's honesty, but also to its continued efforts to respect the dead and wounded. It had been five years since I was carried from the battlefield. Until receiving that letter from the Marine Corps, I had not given my missing backpack any thought.

Following my second year at Duke, a roommate got me a summer job in Birmingham, Alabama, during semester break. While in Alabama, I met and fell in love with Mary Helen Russell, a woman whom I would later marry. Always easily led by a woman's charm, I transferred from Duke University to Birmingham Southern College to be close to her.

Though I was in love, there was always time to fight. Once, a football coach was trying to prevent me from parking in a space. I asked him to back up so I could park my car. He refused and I punched him. The coach showed up for court with a black eye and a swollen lip. The judge stated the mitigating circumstances were considerable, and only ordered me to pay a fine of ten dollars for disorderly conduct.

In the 1950s, there was a popular television show called "Bride and Groom." One day, I called the local station and said I wanted to get married on its show. "Bride and Groom" accepted my offer. As a result, on March 26, 1952, Helen and I drove to New York City and were married on national television. My former Duke University roommate, Byrd, was my best man. The show lavished us with prizes. We received enough furniture to fill a house, a week in the Poconos, and use of a rental car. In addition, they gave my bride a beautiful diamond ring. I took the one I bought her back to the jeweler and got a refund.

After our trip to the Poconos, we returned to New York City, picked up my car, and drove to Winston-Salem, North Carolina, where I resumed my employment with the VA. The marriage came with a bonus—two fine young boys from Helen's previous marriage. I had quite the family, having adopted both boys, Wayne and Jim. We rented an apartment near Baptist Hospital for the first year, and in 1953, I bought my first home, on Ransom Road, in Winston-Salem. We needed the extra space; my family was growing again.

On January 14, 1954, my third son, Louis H. Lucas, II, was born. The first time I held him in my arms, I was amazed and filled with wonder. How would those little hands ever be able to earn a living and what would he grow up to be? I knew the answer; he could aspire to be whatever he wanted. When I held him close, I knew I was experiencing the most wonderful of life's pleasures. While his mother slept, I placed my finger in his tiny hand. His grasp closed tightly around mine and held firm. At that moment this rough and tumble Marine became entwined and bound for life. I realized how my father must have felt the first time he held me in his arms and I hoped beyond measure that he was not disappointed in me.

Looking into my newborn's sleepy blue eyes, I tried very hard to explain to him that I was his dad. He looked somewhat concerned and I could not blame him. I wondered if I could keep him safe and provide him with everything he needed. My heart ached for the parents who had lost their sons in battle. How the parents of the injured must have suffered to bear witness to their once-perfect sons, maimed and forever scarred by the ravages of combat. I could not imagine the pain. Suddenly, my new son made a little sound and my fears were immediately replaced with the newfound warmth of fatherhood.

I whispered to God, "May this child never witness the horrors of battle; for our children's sake, let there be no more wars."

On November 10, 1954, I took my wife and three sons, Wayne, Jimmy, and Louis, to Washington, DC. The occasion was the unveiling and dedication of the Iwo Jima Memorial, or as it is officially titled, The United States Marine Corps War Memorial. President Dwight Eisenhower and Vice President Richard Nixon were there, as well as the last three surviving flag raisers, Ira Hayes, John Bradley, and Rene Gagnon. All through my life there would be events like this, side trips taking me back to the time and place I earned the medal.

In an effort to press forward and complete my education, I took a leave of absence from my job at the Veterans Administration to concentrate fully on school. As a result, in 1956, I received my degree in Business Administration from North Carolina's High Point University. I explored various business ventures, and though I enjoyed some successes in that area, I missed the Marines. After much soul searching, I made the decision to return to the life I enjoyed best—the military.

13

Captain Bam Bam

Facing fear is where courage comes from.

—Jack H. Lucas

In 1961, I went to the Pentagon to look up an old friend, a fellow Medal of Honor recipient, who was highly placed in the US Army. I had hopes of continuing my career in the Marine Corps. However, the opportunity for advancement was too limited in the few Marine Corps Airborne Reconnaissance Units and the army seemed a better fit for my needs. I had a family to consider and income was an issue. I chose to join the paratroopers for a couple of reasons; the position afforded me an increase in salary and it would force me to face my only remaining fear, my fear of heights.

I was commissioned as a first lieutenant in the United States Army on June 5, 1961, and assigned to Fort Benning, Georgia, for basic paratrooper training and officer refresher course. This was a requirement in as much as I had never been an officer. I went through four months training before being sent to Fort Bragg, North Carolina, to serve in the 187th Brigade of the 82nd Airborne Division.

I made forty-five jumps while at Bragg. Most were uneventful, though there was one that is particularly memorable. Typically, ten minutes before reaching a jump site, the plane's door opens. In a few more moments come the commands. "Stand up . . . hook up . . . and check equipment." "Hook up" refers to attaching the tether leading from the parachute to a stationary cable affixed to the plane's interior. When a paratrooper is instructed to "check equipment," he examines the backpack of the trooper in front of him for any irregularities. The checklist includes an examination of your own reserve chute, attached to your front midsection. In addition, a visual check is made to ensure the tether that connects your fellow trooper's chute to the stationary cable, is not encumbered in any way. The tether automatically pulls the primary ripcord when the trooper jumps from the plane.

When the "ready" command is ordered, the first trooper stands in the open doorway in "jump position," which requires placing both hands on the reserve chute, in the event its use is required. Beside the door is a beaming red light. When the pilot has the plane over the drop zone, he flips a switch to turn on a green light. The first man cannot actually see the green light and therefore must be told when it is time to jump. The first man jumps, followed by the remainder of paratroopers, one after another.

One night, while preparing to jump from 1,200 feet, I conducted a thorough check of my gear. I carefully took every necessary precaution. I moved toward the door, and at the precise moment, jumped out into space. I was the last man out. In my head I counted, *One thousand, two thousand, three thousand, four,* and anticipated the familiar "jerk" that occurs when the chute captures the air and blossoms. But there was no jerk. I felt nothing but the sense of my body falling through the atmosphere freely. Looking upward, I saw the chute intertwined and trailing above me like a giant streamer. Reaching up over my head, I grabbed the twisted risers and desperately attempted to spread them apart. If successful, my body would rotate sharply, untwisting the fouled risers, and the chute would blossom, producing a safe descent to the ground below. I was not successful in my attempts and the ground was getting closer and closer.

I gripped the handle on my reserve chute and pulled sharply. The reserve chute deployed, instantly wrapping itself around the primary chute and my head, like a clinging vine. Both chutes had failed to blossom. My only remaining option was to keep my body as loose as possible and do my best to perform a proper parachute landing upon hitting the ground. I would not allow myself to look down, for fear I would stiffen up and break every bone in my body on impact. Forcing myself to relax, I repeated, "Hang loose . . . hang loose." The seconds ticked by and I wondered if they were my last. The situation appeared hopeless. I had faced probable death before, but I had never had so much time to think about it.

To give myself the best chance of surviving the drop, I descended with my toes pointed toward the earth, so immediately upon landing, I would know when to proceed into a roll. If successful, this course of action would decrease the amount of shock to my body. Again, I said to myself, "Hang loose, you can do it Jack! Hang loose." My body impacted the earth hard. I rolled onto my left side and, with the momentum, I bounded up on one knee, a proper parachute landing. I was the last man out of the plane and the first to land.

It took a moment for my mind to absorb everything that had just happened to me. I was shaken, but un-injured. I was glad to be alive. I spoke to the heavens, "Thanks again, God." Despite this incident, I never hes-itated on later jumps. None of those jumps proved as eventful.

I continued to receive official invitations to grand events. On May 19, 1962, President John F. Kennedy had a marvelous birthday celebration and political fund-raiser at Madison Square Garden. Twenty thousand guests were there, some paying as much as one thousand dollars each to attend. It was a night filled with stars; Frank Sinatra was master of ceremonies. The audience bore witness to an array of celebrities including Dean Martin, Jimmy Durante, Peggy Lee, and Ella Fitzgerald. Lena Horne danced with me; she was beautiful. One of the most famous performances in entertainment history occurred that evening. Marilyn Monroe stepped onstage in a rhinestone-studded evening gown and sang, "Happy Birthday, Mr. President." It was spectacular.

During the time I served in the United States Army, I acquired the moniker, "Captain Bam Bam." If someone asked for a fight, I never gave him the opportunity to hit me first; "bam bam" and it was over. A one-two punch was an excellent attitude adjuster. To a point, I had enjoyed being in the army. However, because of my bitter disappointment at being denied combat duty in Vietnam, and my propensity to get into fights, I decided it was best for everyone that I separate from military service. My family and I were stationed at Fort Ord, California, when my discharge became effective on February 21, 1965.

I was in need of employment and a friend of Bob Bush offered me a job in the meat business in Fresno, California. Bob Bush was a fellow Medal of Honor recipient from the state of Washington. We had been friends since we were decorated together in 1945. I had a family to support and this opportunity would provide an income and a new career.

My ultimate goal was to end up with permanent employment on the East Coast. Since my new circumstances required that I frequently move from one location to another, my wife and our boys returned home to Winston-Salem, North Carolina, in anticipation that I would eventually follow. Events I could have never anticipated prohibited my ever joining them again.

I was working in Houston when I decided to try out some of the local nightlife. Gilley's was the place to party in Houston and that is exactly where this ol' party boy headed. I was ordering another drink the first time I laid eyes on her. Yeah boy, she was one fine looking piece of machinery. I watched her wait tables, just so I could admire the view as she walked away. She said her name was Erlene Muckleroy and she was filling in for a friend who was off for the night. Before I knew it, I had allowed myself to become attached to two women at the same time. It was a heart-wrenching position in which to be. The internal struggle caused me immeasurable mental anguish. I deserved it, but these two women did not. Nor did the children. Eventually, my first wife had enough of the situation and we got divorced. She took everything of value, including the kids. All of them. They lived in North Carolina and I lived with my new family all over the United States, wherever my work took me. Having to give up my three boys from my first marriage would haunt me all my life. Erlene and I married, a union that over time would produce two children, a boy, Kelly Lucas, and a girl, Peggy Lucas.

I opened five meat shops in the metropolitan area of Washington, DC, and my business thrived. Erlene and I raised our own beef on a ranch in Maryland and sold fresh cuts to order. Everyone worked hard. My children labored on the farm, caring for the cattle. Erlene and I co-managed the business. Financial responsibilities were primarily hers; I handled logistics.

Our schedules were full every day. Occasionally, when I came home from work, I noticed significant amounts of money lying around the house and I finally admonished Erlene for her negligence. She said she did not have time to do all her chores and had simply failed to deposit the money. Erlene did have a lot of duties, helping out in all aspects of the business, so nothing more on the matter was said. One day, my accountant called and asked me to come in and see him. The news he had for me was not good. He had discovered Erlene was stealing from the company. We perused the company's records together as he explained how he came to that conclusion. When I saw the missing amounts, I was furious. I rushed home and began an all-out search for the stolen money.

From one room to the next I looked for any hidden cash and finally located large amounts in the basement of our house. I confronted Erlene and promptly revoked her financial privileges with the company. Not long after, the accountant notified me that a whole quarter of my records had been lost. Over time, Erlene's actions caused us many problems with the Internal Revenue Service. Years passed before the entire mess was resolved.

My relationship with Erlene was more troubled than

I had first realized. One Sunday afternoon Erlene and I were at home when the phone rang. A concerned voice on the other end of the line inquired, "Mr. Lucas?" I responded, "Yeah." He further inquired, "Are you Mr. Jack Lucas, the owner of the meat stores?" A little perturbed at having been asked twice, I brusquely confirmed I was indeed the Mr. Lucas he was looking for. The caller said, "Mr. Lucas, this is the Maryland State Police. Our office received a complaint this evening concerning some beef purchased at one of your stores. I would appreciate it if you would come to the station right away so we may discuss the problem further."

The request struck me as odd. If someone had indeed filed a complaint, it hardly seemed the sort of thing that would be handled by the state police. After a short exchange to determine the location of our intended meeting, I hung up the receiver.

As she descended the stairs, Erlene asked, "Who was that on the phone?" I looked up at her and briefly conveyed the caller's message, at the same time fumbling for the keys to my Lincoln. With an odd expression of satisfaction on her face, she nodded in the affirmative, and I left the house.

As I walked to my car, I was distracted by how nice our home looked. It was an impressive estate, bordered by beautiful arborvitae and sporadically dotted with many tall blue spruce trees. I had planted each with my own hands and took a great deal of pride in the results. We had a magnificent house, a century-old antebellum mansion with high ceilings, six-thousand square feet of living space, large airy rooms, and lavish fireplaces. I was living the American dream. I had a family, made a good living, and owned nice cars and a luxurious motor home. After years of hard work, I had money in the bank—a lot of money. I was quite pleased with my accomplishments. *Yeah*, I thought, *Jack, ol' boy, you've done all right for a North Carolina farm boy.*

A fog had begun to roll in along the highway, like an ominous forecast of things to come. Erlene's juggling of the books was not the only problem the two of us were having. I had begun to work too hard, drink too much, and spread myself too thin. I had always made my own rules and age did little to change that. As a result, our twenty-year relationship suffered, and we gradually grew apart. She must have felt it too. I began to notice that even during our most private moments she had a different look about her, as if she were hiding something. I had not seen love in her eyes in a very long time. A lot had been sacrificed to build a life with her and I felt it was all slipping away.

I walked into the state police station, identified myself, and was greeted by a state trooper. We went into a small office and he introduced me to another trooper who held a higher rank. I shook his hand and took a seat facing him. He sighed and seemed awfully ill at ease, considering I should have been the uncomfortable one. I sensed that he was about to deliver some bad news. He hesitated and my mind raced to determine what the problem might be. The trooper said, "Mr. Lucas, someone has made a threat against your life." I tried to steady myself for what else he had to tell me. However, there is nothing that could have prepared me for his reply when I asked, "Who?" He responded, "Mr. Lucas, it was your wife."

14

The Ultimate Betrayal

Nobody has ever been so big to me that I felt
out of place. When you start feeling you are not
as good as others, that is when you are insecure.
—Jack H. Lucas

I stared at the trooper for a moment, absolutely stunned
at the prospect that the woman I was living with wanted
me dead. Slowly, the pieces began to fall in place. I knew
Erlene was angry at having been removed from all my
accounts, but I did not realize how angry until that very
moment.

"Mr. Lucas, Mr. Lucas!" the trooper in charge repeated in an effort to bring me back to the matter at

hand. He began to explain. A man had informed the state police of his direct knowledge that individuals were conspiring to have me killed. This man had initially been approached to assist in the murder but refused to be involved. I recognized the name of the informant as a former employee of mine, Larry Melvin. The trooper went on to describe the plan to kill me. He made reference to a man named Jerry Morgan. I told the trooper that Becky Morgan, one of Erlene's daughters from a prior marriage, was married to Jerry. About four months before the couple, along with their baby, had come to live with us, Jerry was in need of employment, so I gave him a job in one of my stores and a pickup truck to drive.

The trooper concluded that Jerry and Erlene had conspired to murder me and make my death look like a suicide. Their scheme hit a snag when Jerry approached my employee, Larry, for help. Larry wanted no part of the deal, and soon after, moved out of town. It was not long before it occurred to Larry that even without his help Erlene and Jerry could still intend to harm me. Larry went to the authorities.

Maryland State Police had a plan of their own. They asked Larry to assist in a sting operation to catch Erlene and Jerry. It was scheduled for the following night, Monday, June 27, 1977. Preliminary details were worked out between the state police, Larry, and me. I would receive further instructions on Monday. Before I left the station, I was advised by the authorities not to return home that night, as my safety could not be guaranteed. I explained that I had to return or my wife would become suspicious. Besides, no one was going to keep me away from my home. After being cautioned to be on my guard, I walked out and headed to my car.

On the drive home, I rewound the last two hours and played them over in my head. Earlier in the day, when I had told Erlene of the complaint filed with the state police about my beef, a faint smile had crept across her face. It seemed strange to me at the time; it was nothing for her to smile about. After I talked to the police, I realized how well that little incident fit into her overall plan. To anyone investigating my suicide, it would seem that I was distraught over the beef complaint. That fact, coupled with our financial problems, would appear to have simply pushed me over the edge. It would seem as though I died by my own hand. Erlene would grieve her way through my checkbook and Jerry would start driving my town car instead of the pickup I loaned him.

I pulled into my residence slowly, rounded the circular drive, and came to a gradual stop by my front door. Stepping from the vehicle, I thought about how tough the last couple of hours had been and how much tougher things would get before this nightmare ended. I was going to have to pull off the performance of a lifetime and do it without any rehearsals or retakes. The biggest challenge was to do it convincingly while feeling hurt and angry as hell.

As I got into bed I thought about Jerry Morgan and his wife under the same roof as me. Lying beside me, in the bed we shared, was my wife. Before I turned out the light, I rolled over and looked into her eyes. The eyes looking back had no love for me; they were dead, lifeless eyes. I had no doubt what I'd learned was true. As I watched Erlene fall asleep, I felt the last vestiges of our marriage slip away, forever. I slept like a baby beside her, all night long. I was not concerned that Erlene and Jerry would kill me in my own home. If they had the guts to do it themselves they would not be out trying to find someone to do it for them.

I later realized fortune had stepped in and saved me just twenty-four hours before I was informed of the plan to assassinate me. The original plan was to kill me on Saturday night, when unexpectedly, my brother showed up from Newport News, Virginia, to spend some time with me. He spoiled their scheme.

On Monday, in accordance with the design laid out

by the state police, Larry, the informant, went to Jerry and told him he had changed his mind and now wanted to participate in the "hit." However, Larry explained, he was too scared to do it himself and had found a hit man to carry out the murder for him. Larry introduced the hit man to Jerry and the plan to kill me got a green light. Jerry did not know the "hit man" was an undercover officer for the Maryland State Police. Jerry agreed to pay the man six thousand dollars up front and an additional amount after the job was completed.

During the day, state police officials contacted me and gave me the details of the operation. They warned me that an attempt would be made to drug me that very night. Jerry Morgan intended to slip me a sedative and take me to my ranch for the execution. The authorities promised to take every precaution for my safety, but I was advised to be on the alert for the unexpected.

Payday for my employees was every Monday. There was typically an accompanying party in the evening at one of my stores, and I was always in attendance. On this occasion—the day of the attempted murder—I planned for the company party to be held at my Suitland, Maryland, store. Upon entering the business, I greeted my step-son-in-law, Jerry, and pulled a chair up to a table. The Suitland store had a fifteen-by-twenty walk-in beef cooler. Without being prompted, Jerry disappeared into the chamber. Moments later, he emerged expressionless carrying a brown bottle of beer. I'd been fully informed what to expect by the state police and remained watchful. Through the dark glass, the swirling concoction of milky colored sedative was clearly visible. I excused myself on the pretext of going to the restroom and took the tainted bottle with me. Undetected, I promptly switched it with another beer I had planted earlier in a desk drawer. Returning to my seat, I pretended to be succumbing to the effects of the drugs. I made little clockwise circles with my head, blinked my eyes, and simulated a struggle to keep them open. I knew Jerry was watching me closely for signs the drug was taking effect and I played my part well. I nodded my head a few times before bringing the act to a close by dropping my head hard on the table, pretending to "pass out." My arms dropped to my side, swung slightly, and eventually became perfectly still. It was the performance of a lifetime. Audie Murphy, eat your heart out!

It was shortly before midnight and the other employees had already gone home. As soon as I was "out," Jerry brought the undercover officer into the store. One of them picked my head up off the table, and together they attempted to lift my body from the chair. It was not an easy task. I was extra-large, heavy, and limp. Jerry grabbed me by one shoulder and the undercover officer, the other. They struggled to get me out of my chair, turning it over in the process. In their efforts, a beer bottle was knocked off a shelf and it shattered across the floor, spreading broken glass in all directions. I was dragged through the shards, which delivered a fair number of cuts and scrapes to my legs and knees. Jerry looked outside to make sure no one was around and swung open the door. Holding me by my upper body, they lugged me through the door and down the front steps of the store. I continued to play dead through the entire ordeal. I felt the toes of my shoes smack the edge of each concrete step all the way down the stairs. The two men carried me in such a way that had they dropped me, I would have fallen flat on my face.

They placed me headfirst in the backseat of my powder-blue Lincoln, which was parked by the front door. I felt my pockets being rifled through in an apparent attempt to obtain keys to the ignition. We were a good fifty yards from the nearest street, Suitland Road. Any activity was too far away to be noticed by passersby. That time of night, traffic was sparse, mostly limited to vehicles coming and going to Andrews Air Force Base. Jerry slammed the car door, nearly pinning my feet in the jam. He then jumped in behind the wheel and the under-cover officer slid in the back passenger seat beside me. I had been dumped partly on the floorboard with my head on the backseat leaning toward the officer. Jerry cranked the car and spun out of the parking lot, the rear end of the vehicle fishtailing out of the turn onto Suitland Road. I wanted to thump his skull for treating my car that way, but I held still as we headed in the direction of my cattle ranch.

The ride from my store to the ranch was about twenty miles. While Jerry drove to the location of my planned murder, unseen officers kept a vigilant watch on my vehicle. A police helicopter hovered overhead, close enough to observe, but not be observed. All air traffic had been diverted, so as not to interfere with the chopper's flight plan. At least eighteen patrol cars alternated tailing my vehicle, to avoid being detected by Jerry. In addition, the undercover policeman sitting beside me was wired for sound and being monitored throughout the operation.

Somewhere along the route, the undercover officer lit a cigarette. Jerry told him, "It's a good thing he's knocked out; he don't like nobody smoking in his car." I wanted to laugh. Jerry was concerned about smoking in my car but not shooting me in it. I felt my belly begin to jiggle. I managed, with no small amount of difficulty, to suppress an audible chuckle. The officer reached over and tapped me on the head, admonishing me to keep quiet.

We arrived at the farm and were met by the informant, Larry. The undercover officer told Larry to keep an eye on me. Then, he and Jerry got into Larry's two-door sports car and drove away to meet Erlene, leaving Larry and me alone on the farm. As soon as Larry gave me the "all clear" and I was sure we were alone, I got up. Larry and I sat quietly in the backseat of my Lincoln and waited.

Erlene had stationed herself about three miles from the farm. Parked in front of a convenience store, in the small town of Old Bowie, Maryland, she sat in her dark green Lincoln waiting for Jerry Morgan and his hired killer. As soon as Jerry and the undercover policeman arrived, Erlene nodded and approached their vehicle. In her grasp, an object was concealed. She reached through Jerry's window, unfolded her hands, and revealed the hidden article. In her palm rested my .38 caliber revolver. The one and same revolver my mother stuck in the sharecropper's ribs when he broke into our house and the one I spun around my finger like Wild Bill Hickock and shot through my tent in Linda Vista, California. They planned to shoot me in the mouth with my own gun to better sell my execution as a suicide to the authorities.

With the would-be murder weapon in hand, the undercover policeman and Jerry drove away and headed back to my location. As soon as they were out of sight, law enforcement officers converged on Erlene. Her turning the weapon over to the hit man left no doubt of her intent and she was immediately arrested. Meanwhile, back at the ranch, Larry and I were still sitting in the backseat awaiting the return of Jerry and the officer. The moon was still in its first quarter, and from where my car was sitting, under a huge shady tree, the world looked pretty dark. Off in the distance we saw a car turn off the highway. Approaching headlights were visible, slowly winding their way up the long gravel drive in our direction. Larry and I did not talk. We sat anxiously anticipating what was about to occur. Jerry Morgan and his hired man slowly pulled up beside us. Jerry must have been surprised to see two heads visible in my car. After all, I was supposed to be knocked out in the backseat. He stopped his car and stared at us for a moment or two. As Jerry tried to calculate his next move, the undercover officer drew his service weapon, stuck it into Jerry's right cheek, and said, "You're under arrest, you son of a bitch!"

More officers arrived on the scene, cuffed Jerry, and

took him into custody. There was some small satisfaction in witnessing his arrest. However, to have had my life threatened—and by my wife—was devastating and extremely painful. Had I been as mad as I was hurt, I would have killed someone.

The story was making the national news and front pages of every major newspaper. The entire debacle was extremely hard on our children. Erlene was in jail, where she would stay for about six weeks. I did not desire to speak to her, not even when I took our children to see her on visitation day. Eight-year-old Peggy and nine-year-old Kelly were distraught when they saw their mother behind bars. Hearing them cry for her was more than I could stand. At trial, I pleaded to the court on Erlene's behalf. As a result of my request for leniency, she received a reduced sentence of ten years probation instead of the twenty years she was exposed to. Likewise, Jerry received a lighter sentence. I always wondered what Jerry and his wife expected to gain from my death.

Devastated that my wife, someone that I shared so much history with, wanted me dead for monetary gain, I sold my house and set up a doublewide mobile home on the Maryland ranch. Material things held no value for me anymore. Heartbroken and filled with despair, I gave away or sold almost everything I owned. My marriage to Erlene had dissolved. My life was a mess. I would learn to live with the hurt, betrayal, and disappointment, but I would never fully recover from it.

15

Rock Bottom

A man may die, nations may rise and fall, but
an idea lives on.
                            —President John F. Kennedy

Many times over the years, when things were not going
well for me personally, something good would occur to
brighten my spirits. More often than not, that something
had to do with the Medal of Honor. Such was the case
at this point in my life. It was time for the annual Medal
of Honor Convention. I needed some time away, and this
particular year, the convention was held in Hawaii.

I was always known for being somewhat of a rebel. It
took a lot of effort on my part to live up to a reputation

like that, but I managed. While attending the convention in Hawaii, I rented a brand-new Kawasaki motorcycle for the two weeks I planned to be there and I rode all over the island. A fellow Medal of Honor recipient, Jake Lindsey, from the US Army, dared me to take him for a ride through the lobby of the hotel. He climbed on the back and I revved the engine a little, popped the clutch, and headed through the front door. At the very last possible moment, Jake jumped off and sent me in alone. A Marine would have never bailed out on a buddy like that. I rode around the lobby, between the sofas, by the front desk, racing my engine, popping wheelies, and having a good time. I politely left when I realized the spectacular event was not being well received by the hotel staff. I parked my bike outside and returned to the lobby. Everyone was smiling when I walked inside and they shook their heads in disbelief as I passed. I encountered Pappy Boyington when he stepped off the elevator. He had a black eye and a few bruises. I laughed when I saw him. We could be a rowdy bunch. I was glad to have the rest and relaxation after everything that had happened to me, but like all good things, the convention ended and I returned home.

My landlady informed me that my lease on the ranch was not going to be renewed, so I purchased adjoining acreage and moved my mobile home onto it. The residence had electricity, but no water, and though my home was not fully ready for occupancy, my fifteen-year-old son from my second marriage, Kelly, moved in with me. Our daughter, Peggy, continued to live with her mother. The land I was living on had been caught up in some controversy. For some reason that was never clear to me, somebody did not want anyone living there. The previous resident on the property had been a victim of arson shortly before my purchase of it. I was desperately trying to provide some stability for my son and with nowhere else to go, I was determined to hold on to what remained of my life, so I dug in my heels and stood fast.

One spring evening, around midnight, Kelly and I turned in as usual. My nightly routine included checking the locks and turning out all the lights. Lastly, I would lay my hearing aids on the nightstand, before finally rolling over and going to sleep. Nighttime noises and big trucks barreling down the highway in front of my residence did not bother me in the least. To keep from lying awake all night, pondering my problems, I forced myself to think of happier times. It was a relaxing mental exercise, conducive to sleep.

There was a window of a few short years in my life, before I lost my father, when I was absolutely at peace. That is the place I sought in my meditations. I tried to think of family picnics, napping with my puppy under a shady tree, and long walks on the beach with my dad. If sound sleep did not come quickly, my pleasant thoughts were occasionally crowded out by a bad memory and that had a tendency to initiate terrible nightmares. If that happened, I would be fretful in my sleep, thrashing my arms and legs about and talking wildly. As I had never had a problem with nightmares prior to my time on Iwo Jima, I assume the horrors were brought by my resulting physical and mental wounds.

On this particular spring night, I drifted off to sleep harboring memories of a happy neighborhood full of playing children. I dreamt of endless afternoons playing games in the Atlantic sunshine and running down warm dusty roads in my bare feet, a time when the world was a much friendlier place in which to live, a time when the biggest disappointment you had to face was chasing a rainbow after a summer shower only to have it dissipate before you've reached its end.

When I was a little boy, no older than five, I loved to play in a small meadow located down the street from my house. All the kids that lived close by gathered there to occupy themselves. One day, I was in the middle of the field, not paying much attention to the older boys, who had suddenly acquired a typical adolescent interest in matches. As can be expected, things got out of control and the field was soon ablaze. It had been a while since it had rained and the tall grass was prime kindling. I had a clear recollection of the smell of smoke and sharp pops and snaps of the fire devouring the tall dry stalks that grew all around. Before I knew it, a circle of fire surrounded me and I was trapped. The flames shot upward, high over my head. Through the smoke and flames I could not see the other children very well, but I could hear them and the panic in their voices. The older kids desperately beat back the fire in an attempt to save me, a fight they were losing for a while. Several of them began to concentrate their efforts in one area, eventually opening up a clear passage wide enough to make good my escape. I thought I was going to burn alive, but in the last few moments, the boys found the strength and fortitude to set me free.

THE MEMORY MADE me sleep fitfully and I continued to hear the crack of fire and smell the stifling smoke. I awoke suddenly, every one of my senses alerted. Instantly, I knew something was wrong. The room was bright, as if someone's headlights were shining in my windows. I jumped up to investigate. From overhead came a sharp crack of timbers breaking. The pungency of smoke stung my nostrils. I ran out the back door in my skivvies to see what was happening. It was early spring and the night air had a sharp chill to it. Once I rounded the corner and looked toward the front of the house, I saw it. There was a line of fire burning along the ground, parallel to the front of my home. It appeared to have been fueled by an accelerant of some kind. Flames were leaping up around the entire structure. I rapidly beat on the outside wall to wake my son and darted inside to make sure he could get out. There was only enough time to grab the clothes I had worn the day before and a jacket. Kelly and I swiftly exited our home for the last time. The interior was filled with smoke and it was only by God's grace we escaped alive. I had no phone and by the time emergency vehicles were notified and arrived, the structure was fully engulfed; it was a total loss. The only thing that would remain was a garage I had built with my own hands a few steps from my back door. Since my water had not yet been connected, my application for insurance had not been accepted. What was lost was lost.

As the fire blazed, clothes fell from my bedroom closet across a box of personal belongings, snuffing out the flames. As a result, one solitary cardboard box containing a few of my personal effects did not burn. Unfortunately, books, photographs, and my entire collection of records—hundreds of old 45s, 33s, and 78s—were consumed. Worst of all, the closet where I kept my Medal of Honor was completely destroyed.

Two days later, I examined the wreckage that was once my home. The sky was dark and overcast, an accurate reflection of my mood. I stood ankle-deep in the still smoldering remnants and tried to absorb the loss. A breeze whistled in the pines, forecasting its approach, and whipped up the ash in little dust devils all around my feet. With each step, charred timbers snapped and metal siding popped beneath me as I attempted to locate the approximate area of the closet where I had stored my medal. I dropped to my knees in the warm gray ash, carefully sifting through the cinders with my bare hands in hopes of making the recovery. It took only a moment before I felt the star shape resting just a few inches below the surface. Grasping it tightly in my fist, I retrieved it from the ash and inspected it carefully. The ribbon was burned completely away, but every detail of the medal itself was intact. The ribbon could easily be replaced. It is not unusual to need a replacement ribbon. Occasionally they get soiled and fresh ones are issued. Looking upon the face of the medal in my palm, I gently wiped the powdered ash from the image of the goddess Minerva and slowly turned it over. Clearly legible on the reverse was the inscription, *For Action Above and Beyond the Call of Duty in Iwo Jima on 20 Feb 1945*. Carefully, I slipped it into my left breast pocket.

I was physically, mentally, and emotionally exhausted. As a result, I was hospitalized for a while and ultimately diagnosed with Posttraumatic Stress Disorder. It would be many more years before doctors discovered I had shrapnel in the left frontal lobe of my brain. I longed for complete rest and peace in my life. I was on total disability, for which I would receive compensation for the balance of my lifetime. It would not make me a rich man, but it helped me meet my needs, another example of what makes this nation so wonderful and why I have always loved her. I did not forget her when she needed me, and later, once my capabilities were limited, she did not forget me. While in the hospital, I was able to rest, and it was not long before they discharged me. I was never sure if they let me go because I got better or because I punched a patient that was irritating me. Whatever the reason, I went home to my garage.

I surveyed the ruins and asked aloud, "How many times must a man start over?" A voice in my head answered, *As many times as it takes.*

16

Down but Not Out

In life, it's not what you've lost, but what you
have left that counts.

—Hubert H. Humphrey

Except for my garage, I had no place to live. A friend
asked me to help him with a building project near his
farm in Maryland. He said I could pitch a tent on his
land and live there while the project was in progress.
Having nothing better to do at the time, I accepted his
offer, taking along my son, Kelly, a gifted builder in his
own right. I had been on the farm only two weeks when
law enforcement located some marijuana growing on the
property and I was suspected of being involved. I did not

smoke marijuana and had even given up tobacco. The press got a little mileage out of the situation, with headlines such as, "War Hero Charged with Growing Pot." At the time the plants were discovered I had only been living on the property for two weeks. Because the plants found were already full-grown, the charges against me were dropped.

Under the circumstances, I packed up and went home. My son went to live with friends and I moved into the garage I had built behind my mobile home. There was no plumbing or telephone.

I became somewhat of a curiosity to the media and a major network picked up my story. The CBS television news show, "West 57th," came to interview me as an American hero living off the land after suffering hard times. A crew shot some footage of me bathing and shaving outdoors in cold water, water that had to be brought in from elsewhere. My humble living quarters were filmed, along with the small stove I cooked on. The reporter asked me how I felt about life after all that had happened to me. I responded, "I'm down, but I'm coming back."

A veteran in Hattiesburg, Mississippi, saw the nationwide broadcast and invited me to visit him there. While pondering his offer, I looked at the pile of twisted steel and ash that was once my home. A periwinkle vine had attached itself to the steel trailer frame and appeared to be flourishing. It made me think. I could interpret what I saw as renewal, a sign of hope and possibility. More than likely, it was just another parasite sucking what life it could from what little I had left. My decision was made. I bought a truck and new trailer, left the wreckage to the periwinkle vine, and headed south to Mississippi. Once I settled there, I knew I would never leave.

In time, I bought a home in Hattiesburg where I reside today. There were ninety-six virgin pines on my property, enabling me to fell and dress my own lumber to remodel the existing house. With blueprints only in my head, and my very own hands, my home grew from sixteen hundred square feet to four thousand square feet. I built a guesthouse, a structure I call the "honey-hut," right behind my house. Its amenities include a poolroom, bath, and spa. Lastly, I constructed a spacious front porch, in anticipation of my eventual retirement. I found Mississippi to be a warm and friendly place. The people of Hattiesburg became gracious friends and neighbors.

Back home in the little coastal town of Washington, North Carolina, my mother, then in her nineties, had become quite frail and needed constant attention. She wanted no part of life in a nursing home, so her only option was to move to Mississippi where I could better see to her needs. She was living with me in Mississippi when I took a couple days off in 1995 for a trip to Washington, DC.

In January of 1995, President Bill Clinton planned to speak about "continuity and service" in his State of the Union speech on January 24. Hillary Clinton came up with the idea of inviting the youngest American in the twentieth century to have received the Medal of Honor. My second oldest adopted son, Jimmy, was grown, with a teenage son of his own named Matthew Lucas, and living in Winston-Salem, North Carolina. Jimmy was a graduate of West Point and served two tours of duty in Vietnam. A representation of three generations of family, we were considered a good example of continuity and service.

I got a call on Saturday informing me to be in Washington on Monday, in order to prepare for the Tuesday event. Before I left Hattiesburg, I tended to some outside chores that needed immediate attention. A neighbor who knew little about me struck up a conversation and asked me what my plans were for the weekend. I replied, "I'm going up to DC, as a special guest of the president." He looked at me as if I were crazy. I found out later, after we became friends, he went home that day and told his wife he thought I was the biggest liar he had ever heard. I wish I could have seen his face two days later when he saw me on the live broadcast.

By Sunday, all the preparations were made and I caught a plane out of Jackson, Mississippi, on Monday morning. Upon my landing in DC, I was picked up by a White House limousine and taken from the airport to a beautiful hotel on the Potomac River. My son and grandson, who both caught a separate flight out of North Carolina, met me there. We were wined and dined in style at the hotel, before being escorted to the White House late in the afternoon. Officials gave us a private tour of the house and grounds, and allowed us to go wherever we wished. We took a number of pictures before returning to the hotel, where we were wined and dined again.

I had been to the Capitol countless times; each return trip filled my mind with many wonderful memories. Unfortunately, there was always an awful sadness that accompanied them. I viewed the monuments in this memorial-filled city as not only a celebration of the American spirit but also a testament to the cost of freedom. As I laid in my darkened hotel room and saw the radiance of DC glittering in the night through my window, I reflected on a poem I learned in college by the Greek Aeschylus.

Even in our sleep, pain which cannot forget
Falls drop by drop upon the heart,
Until, in our own despair, against our will,
Comes wisdom through the awful grace of God.

I think of them always, my fallen brothers, every day and every night, without fail.

Morning arrived and I realized it was Tuesday—the big day. A limousine drove my son, grandson, and me to the White House. We sat in the driveway and watched the president and Mrs. Clinton enter a limousine in front of us. Security had cleared Pennsylvania Avenue for our procession, and with sirens screaming, we traveled by motorcade to the Capitol. As I stepped into the Capitol entry, the Clintons graciously met us with greetings of warm welcome. The president turned and went one direction while the first lady, my family, and I took the elevator to an upper level. We were seated in the gallery, next to Mrs. Clinton. I told her she was a magnificent looking lady and even prettier in person than on television. She smiled warmly and I could see that beyond her good looks and intelligence, she possessed great poise and grace. Toward the end of his speech, President Clinton looked up at me, and while the entire country listened, he stated

The last person I want to introduce is Jack Lucas, from Hattiesburg, Mississippi. Jack, would you like to stand up?

Fifty years ago in the sands of Iwo Jima, Jack Lucas taught, and learned the lessons of citizenship. On February 20, 1945, he and three of his buddies encountered the enemy and two grenades at their feet. Jack Lucas threw himself on both of them. In that moment, he saved the lives of his companions, and miraculously, in the next instant, a medic saved his life. He gained a foothold for freedom, and at the age of seventeen, just a year older than his grandson, who is up there with him today, and his son, who is a West Point graduate and a veteran, at seventeen, Jack Lucas became the youngest Marine in history . . . to win the Congressional Medal of Honor.

The entire Chamber, which included both Houses of Congress, Supreme Court justices, military leaders, and members of the president's Cabinet, stood, looked up at me, and responded with thunderous applause, a roar that continued for no less than five minutes. I was humbled by the experience. I wanted to smile, but I could not. It was everything I could do to keep from crying. I was completely swept away.

The president continued

> All these years later, yesterday, here is what [Jack Lucas] said about that day. "It didn't matter where you were from, or who you were, you relied on one another." You did it for your country. We all gain when we give, and we reap what we sow. That's at the heart of this New Covenant, responsibility, opportunity and citizenship, more than stale chapters in some remote civics book, they are still the virtue by which we can fulfill ourselves, and reach our God-given potential, and be like them, and also to fulfill the eternal promise of this country, the enduring dream, from that first, and most sacred covenant. I believe every person in this country still believes that we are created equal, and given by our Creator, the right to life, liberty, and the pursuit of happiness.
>
> This is a very, very great country and our best days are still to come.
>
> Thank you and God bless you all.

Following the president's speech, I returned to the lower level of the Capitol, and once again, met with President Clinton. I told him, "Sir, you've got a lot of courage. Every day, no matter what people say, you keep smiling. If I was on a job and somebody criticized me as much as they criticize you, I'd be in the nuthouse." I was thrilled at the opportunity to hug Mrs. Clinton, and the vice president's wife, Tipper Gore. The president, first lady, and Mrs. Gore were gracious enough to allow us many photographs of the occasion. It was interesting to watch the reactions of my son and grandson. To them, I was just Dad and Grandpa. All the attention I was getting left them speechless. I was glad such an occasion arose so that I could share my history with them.

In the days and weeks that followed, I was contacted by many of my old buddies from the service who had seen the State of the Union speech. On the night I was introduced to America—nearly fifty years after my act of heroism—I went back to my hotel room and lay down in bed though I did not sleep. When I spoke to my Lord that night, I told Him how much I appreciated the recognition extended me by the president and first lady. By remembering me they had also remembered my fallen brothers in arms. I wanted each of those men to always be remembered.

The president had quoted me as saying, "It didn't matter where you were from, or who you were, you relied on one another." The statement was heartfelt. Marines had always, and will always, look out for each other, *Semper Fidelis*. Americans need to be reminded of those who sacrificed it all. Had they lived, any one of the men that died on that God-forsaken island would have carried the torch forward, reminding the world of the cost of freedom. However, that honor and privilege fell to me. It is not a responsibility I've taken lightly.

Less than one month after the State of the Union address, I was back in Washington, DC, to commemorate the fiftieth anniversary of the Battle of Iwo Jima. Hillary Clinton invited me to the White House, where she presented me with an enlarged photo of my family standing beside her, which had been taken during our last visit to the Capitol. It was a nice gesture on her part and something I would always treasure.

February 19, 1995, was clear and brisk. I was chauffeured to the Iwo Jima Memorial for the commemoration. We were a sizeable group. I was accompanied by my son, Jimmy, who attended the State of the Union address the month before; my first biological son, Louis Harold, and his family; my daughter Peggy; and a grandson,

Jowjie Lucas. Cast after the most famous photo of World War II, and towering nearly eighty feet above us, stood the huge bronze tribute to the Marine Corps. I took my place in front of the Marines standing atop Mount Suribachi, ever vigilant of their nation's flag raised on the morning of February 23, 1945. I have stood here many times over the years and my pride has never waned. On this particular visit, a red carpet had been rolled out at the base of the monument. I had the honor of walking down the carpeted runway alongside Captain Robert Dunlap—the same man I'd surrendered to aboard the USS *Deuel* fifty years before.

It was a grand event to share with the president. I looked up at the gargantuan Marines, their images forever frozen in the struggle to raise the flag on the volcano's summit. It was a fitting symbol of the triumph of free men. No one said it better than Admiral Chester Nimitz: "Among the Americans who fought on Iwo Jima, uncommon valor was a common virtue." General "Howlin' Mad" Smith, commander of Iwo Jima's assault force added, "It was the most savage, and the most costly, battle in the history of the Marine Corps."

A young man had to be physically as well as mentally fit to be a Marine and undergo rigorous and extensive training. Therefore, when a Marine died in battle, America was giving up the best she had. The power of the structure was astounding; it embodied the American spirit. Emotion weighed heavy on my heart. God, I loved the Marines.

17

Winds of Change

Do not judge me by my beginning, only by my
end; nor by the path I took, but where it led me.

—Jack H. Lucas

My mother lived with me for four years, during which
time she suffered a stroke and was rendered completely
helpless. I watched over her daily, only leaving her with
a sitter for as long as it took to see about household concerns. I saw to her every want and need. She had to be
physically lifted and carried wherever she needed to go.
Though I enjoyed preparing her favorite dishes and fuss-
ing over her, the demands of her care began to take a toll
on me physically and emotionally. My doctor advised it

was time to make other arrangements. Regrettably, I began seeking outside facilities for her care.

Mother wanted to go home to North Carolina, where she could be laid to rest beside my father, from whom we were so painfully separated many years before. I visited her there several times a year and was by her side during her final days. She was in her nineties. I asked her once, "What is your secret to living such a long life?" She replied, "Keep breathing, son. Keep breathing." She held on to life as long as she could. In the end, her body simply gave out.

The winds of change had relocated the place I call home from North Carolina to Mississippi. All my life God had been a constant guide, tugging first in one direction, then another, directing me on a straighter path than the one I had a tendency to follow. In 1998, it became abundantly clear to me why fate had sent me to Hattiesburg. One day, a pleasant and delightful woman walked into my life. She was pretty, smart, and possessed the virtue of unlimited patience. Her name was Ruby Clark, and when she agreed to marry me, I knew I had finally found the woman I would spend the rest of my life with.

My marriage to Ruby has provided me a peace in my life like I have never known. We have traveled to many events and speaking engagements together, and over the years, she has learned to put up with most of my faults. In return, she has received my undying love and devotion.

What Ruby and I have enjoyed most are the trips we have taken together. She accompanied me on a trip to Indianapolis to help dedicate a war memorial in the city. Medal of Honor recipients circled the Indianapolis Speedway as a crowd of thousands of cheering fans stood and waved to us as we passed by. Schools were closed so that children could attend the memorial dedication. Twenty-five thousand students showed up and waited for hours for an opportunity to meet the medal recipients. I was told it was time to leave the gathering at 1600 hours, but I refused. As long as there were children wanting to see me, I would make myself available to them. The line of people waiting stretched as far as the eye could see. Officials asked my wife if she could persuade me to leave so the crowd would disperse and I could go on to the next event. She responded, "Not as long as there is a child remaining." For two more hours I visited with children, shook hands, and signed autographs. I knew if I turned my back on a child, he would never forget it, or forgive me.

My wife graciously agreed to accompany me to Ingall's Shipyard in Pascagoula, Mississippi, at the invitation of shipbuilder, and former Marine captain, Andy Harmon. The purpose of the trip was to view the construction of a new assault ship, the USS *Iwo Jima* (LHD-7). When I first saw her, she was in five big pieces. Once completed, she would stretch 844 feet in length, displace over forty thousand tons, and carry a complement of thirty helicopters and up to eight Harriers. The new ship had a capacity of 1,086 ship's company men and 1,897 Marine Corps troops.

Well before her christening and launch date of March 25, 2001, a ceremony took place called "stepping the mast." During the ceremony, items of historical significance were placed in the mast of the ship. The items would remain there through the life of the vessel. Officials presented me with a book about my life, containing many photos and articles, to be placed in the mast during this ceremony. Another book about the 5th Marine Division and coins contributed by the commandant of the Marine Corps were among additional items.

When the navy completed running her through all the necessary trials, she was ready to be commissioned on June 30, 2001. I was invited to sail with the *Iwo* from Pascagoula to Pensacola, Florida, for the event. Some of my Marine Corps League buddies went with me. There was a drenching rain the day of USS *Iwo Jima*'s (LHD-7) commissioning, but no spirits were dampened.

I have attended numerous proceedings aboard the LHD-7 as a special guest and have been privileged to speak to graduating naval officers in Pensacola as well. I am grateful to Captain John Nawrocki for his having made me part of the USS *Iwo Jima*. To this day, he remains a close friend of mine. I am known to the navy as "Uncle Jack," a title that means a great deal to me. I hope they think of me as family, because that is exactly how I feel about them.

Since I first arrived on this world in 1928, the elements of my life have changed many times, varying jobs, friends, family, and even where I consider "home" to be. The one constant that has kept me anchored through the years has been the steadfast relationship between me and the United States Marine Corps.

My travels have taken me far away, as far as Iwo Jima itself. Due to its remoteness, Iwo Jima is the most difficult battlefield of World War II to visit. It is nearly abandoned, home only to a Japanese military defense post. Upon my first return to the island, I scouted some of the subterranean tunnels and took a film crew on a tour of one. As we descended deeper and deeper into the bowels of the island, the temperature rose drastically. The air was stifling hot and moist, like a sauna. The film crew asked me if I was sure I knew where I was going. I laughed and assured them with a confident, "Of course I do." I had absolutely no idea how to get out, but I knew the tunnels had multiple apertures, and sooner or later, I would locate one.

Ultimately, I discovered an opening, long overgrown with the dense ugly foliage that grew on the island. Its location had been revealed by a faint ray of light filtering into the tunnel from overhead. I poked my head above ground, turned to the film crew and instructed, "Here's how you get out." I further explained, "I merely wanted to demonstrate how these tunnels wound around under the surface, then opened up in various locations." Throughout my explanation, the crew was climbing through the black ash, getting themselves, and their valuable equipment, absolutely filthy. I can only imagine what they were thinking and what they said about me when I was out of earshot.

I contracted something while in the caves and began to cough relentlessly. My discomfort intensified until I feared I would suffocate. I was immediately flown, along with the Marine Band, to the island of Okinawa. Upon arrival, I was placed in the naval hospital where I remained in intensive care for eight days. Once well enough to be released, it was my intention to catch a flight to the Philippines to visit my oldest son, Wayne, stationed at Clark Air Force Base, but it was not to be. I suffered a relapse at Subic Bay and was immediately flown home. That was the second time Iwo Jima nearly cost me my life.

In 2001, I returned to Iwo Jima again and participated in a venture to produce a documentary, "Price for Peace," about the war in the Pacific. I took my wife, Ruby, along with me on this occasion to allow her to better understand this important chapter in my life. I used our time on the island to show Ruby where I landed on Red Beach One, and from atop Mount Suribachi, pointed out the approximate location of the trench where I covered the two grenades with my body. Unfortunately, the site was covered in thick undergrowth that rendered the exact location inaccessible. I had not kept myself well hydrated on this visit and became sick enough to be hospitalized in Guam where I was put on intravenous fluids until I was well enough to travel home.

My history of bad luck with Iwo Jima did not deter me from returning once more for the Sixtieth Anniversary Reunion in March 2005. I was accompanied by my writer, Dorea Kuck Drum. We had already retraced the steps of my life, beginning with the house where I was born and the town I grew up in. We had shared trips to Washington, DC, to perform research and to Norfolk, Virginia, to witness USS *Iwo Jima*'s Captain John Snedeker rename the Harrier flight deck the PFC Jacklyn H. Lucas Airfield. It was fitting for us to visit Iwo Jima together in order to produce the best possible historical record of my action there.

Except for a wreath-laying ceremony, where the tardiness of the Japanese delegation kept Americans waiting in the hot sun for a lengthy period, our time was our own. Once again, I stood on Mount Suribachi and retraced my steps visually from Red Beach One to Airfield One where I encountered the grenades. I felt many emotions: grief, for the loss and waste of life, and anger, brought on by still-lingering contempt for the enemy, combined with sheer satisfaction and joy that we had kicked butt.

I relished my time with the Iwo Jima veterans and the young Marines to whom the awesome responsibility of protecting our nation has been passed. I posed for pictures and signed numerous autographs. Due to the injuries I sustained on Iwo, there is nerve damage and limited flexibility of my wrist and fingers. As a result, my shaky signature takes some time to complete and my salute has a tendency to appear somewhat cavalier, but they are the best I can do.

THE SUN BEGAN to fade into the peaceful indigo Pacific. I stood alone on the infamous Red Beach, the coarse volcanic ash crunching beneath my feet with each slight shift of my weight. With the exception of the small Japanese outpost, the island was desolate. I listened intently for any lingering echoes of battle, but instead, heard only the wind and peaceful surf, lapping upon the deserted shore. The words of an unknown author came to mind.

> *War drew us from our homeland in the*
> *sunlit springtime of our youth.*
> *Those who did not come back alive*
> *remain in perpetual springtime—forever young*
> *and a part of them is with us always.*

Standing as straight as my old bones would allow, I threw my shoulders back and set my eyes on the horizon. I strained every muscle in my hand to perform my smartest salute, the ring finger of my right hand inevitably slack and out of line; like me, a little out of line, but constantly striving to get the job done. I snapped my salute at the regulation forty-five degree angle and returned my hand to my side.

I opened my fist and studied the glossy black cinders I had been holding, each one representative of a life never fully lived. American blood was forever embedded in every tiny grain.

I gently tilted my hand and let the grains of ash slowly slip through my fingers and back to earth.

Epilogue

The war is never far away from me, mentally or physically. For the rest of my life I will live with grenade fragments in my brain and lungs, some pieces as big as a .22 round. My right arm is functional, but forever scarred with the discoloration of embedded black ash and numerous surgical procedures. I set off metal detectors at airports and will always be subject to a more thorough check at the gate than others. With fresh batteries in my hearing aids, I can hear as well as anyone, though the ringing in my ears continues to this day. My lungs are my biggest worry, and as I grow older, my joints have needed replacing. Most of my ailments are indicative of the price I paid for peace in the Pacific region.

I know God was, and is, working in my life. He placed me on the one ship out of two hundred anchored in the harbor, where my cousin was on board to help me stow away. He jammed my rifle so that I would look downward and see the grenades at my buddies' feet. He stopped my heavy bleeding when I asked Him to save me. He broke my fall from 1,200 feet when my chute did not open. He persuaded a young man to warn Maryland authorities that my life was in danger. The list goes on and on.

I do not know why God spared my life so many times. I have been searching for an answer to that question since that fateful day in February 1945. I feel that He has entrusted me with the responsibility of passing on to other Americans my firsthand knowledge of the enormous price that has been paid for their freedom. Those who have died on the field of battle cannot speak for themselves; that duty is mine. I will carry their banner forward and continue to plant the seeds, so others may continue the work after I am gone. The honor is humbling.

I have been more honored by the goodwill of people resulting from my having received the Medal of Honor, than by receiving the medal itself. When I was decorated with the Medal of Honor, I did not grow wings and become an angel. I was still the same man I always was and always will be, as imperfect as they come. The men who have worn the medal created its prestige, not the other way around. I am not proud of everything I have done in my life, quite the contrary. Some of my behavior is disappointing, not only to others, but to myself as well. However, I have never brought shame to the Medal of Honor and pray I never do. I must not, for it represents far too much.

Only by the grace of God have I had the privilege of accepting accolades and glory for my actions. Other men have performed bravely, even given their lives for their country, but did not survive to receive the gratitude of their nation. Their acts were witnessed only by God Almighty Himself. I pray their reward is more glorious than any we can imagine.

I had the tenacity to go after the enemies of my nation, to stand up for this country, having never rationalized about an imposed age limit or regulation. I have proven that anyone can step up and make a difference, as long as they have the determination and perseverance to stick to their goals and forge ahead, regardless of any obstacles. As long as we have people of faith, vision, and patriotic spirit there is the prospect of a marvelous future for our country. Pride in America will help us sustain the unprecedented liberties we know and enjoy. Freedom did not come cheaply, nor does it have a guarantee to last. It carries with it responsibilities of each and every one of us. You must be driven if you aspire to succeed. There is not much left for me to aspire to at my age, but to have a successful book written so I may tell people my story. I also aspire to sit and rock on the magnificent porch I built on the front of my home in Mississippi, and when my story has been told, that is precisely what I am going to do.

Afterword to the William Morrow Paperback Edition

by D. K. Drum

Jack sat on that front porch enjoying the southern breeze until this book was released. The demand for public appearances increased exponentially. He enjoyed the people, especially the veterans and children, and never turned down a request to attend an event, as long as his body allowed.

His last public appearance was where it all began, at Parris Island. Shortly thereafter, in the spring of 2008, Jack found out from his doctor that he had not only more shrapnel damage to his body than was known before, but also leukemia. Every day I watched him become weaker, and his health demanded he spend more time at home.

One morning, he was sitting at his dining room table, which was typically surrounded by friends and visitors, with just my husband, Tommy, and me. We were watching him try to finish an autograph on a copy of his book. While still holding his pen, he called to his wife, "Ruby, baby, I can't do anymore." She walked over, rubbed his back and responded, "Honey, you've done enough," and she took the book and pen away. My husband and I hurt much more than we let anyone know. We fought back tears; Tommy and I loved Jack to no end. We knew he was making every effort to be strong. He stood up straight, reminding me of an old lion walking proudly through the savanna, even though he knew his time was running short.

Two days later, he entered the hospital in Hattiesburg, Mississippi. For several days, medical professionals did everything possible to extend his life. His friends and wife stayed with him during the day. He was never alone, and we knew he felt our love. A minister entered his room one evening, touched his back, and told him, "Jack, God has His hand on your shoulder." I had the night watch so his wife could go home and get some rest. Standing by his bed, I hummed a hymn for a couple of hours. I remember it was "Nearer, My God, to Thee." Fifteen minutes past midnight, on June 5, 2008, as he was fighting fiercely for every last breath of life, I held his hand tightly. However, like the old lion on the Serengeti, he was resigned that the time had come for him to join those heroes, his brothers in arms. He closed his eyes for the last time, his duty done.

On May 7, 2018, construction began on a guided missile destroyer in Pascagoula, Mississippi. The vessel is scheduled to be launched in 2023, the assigned name . . .

The USS *Jack H. Lucas.*

Jack and Ruby Lucas, April 2008.

Index

About the Authors

JACKLYN "JACK" HAROLD LUCAS enlisted in the United States Marine Corps on August 6, 1942, at the age of fourteen. He was assigned to the 1st Battalion, 26th Marine Regiment, 5th Marine Division during the Battle of Iwo Jima. He received the Medal of Honor from President Harry S. Truman on October 5, 1945. After graduating from college, he enlisted in the United States Army in 1961 and served four years in the 82nd Airborne Division. He was married to Ruby Lucas and they lived in Hattiesburg, Mississippi. He passed away in 2008 at the age of eighty.

Inspired by parents who were part of the "greatest generation" and a brother who received the Bronze Star in Vietnam and later succumbed to his wartime injury, D. K. DRUM collaborated with Jack Lucas to write *Indestructible*. She is married to thrice-decorated Vietnam veteran Tommy Drum. The price paid for freedom is an important lesson that has been forwarded on to their progeny: Jon, Laura, Isabel, Juliana, and Willa. May the torch burn brightly as it is passed to all future generations.